APPLY THE LAW OF ATTRACTION

*Inspiration And Navigation
For Deliberate Creators*™

LES GOODRICH

Apply The Law of Attraction:
Inspiration And Navigation For Deliberate Creators

Copyright © 2014 by Leslie Ernest Goodrich.

All rights reserved.

The contents of this book may not be copied or reproduced (except in instances of brief attributed quotations published for editorial review) without the prior written permission of the author: Goodrich, Leslie E. (05-01-2014).

Published by
DV8NOW Publishing
Vero Beach, FL

www.dv8now.com

Free LOA Blog & Newsletter at
espressoforyourgoals.com

Table of Contents

Introduction v

Chapter 1: A Paradigm Shift 11

Chapter 2: Destination (Ideal Desired Result) 23

Chapter 3: Visualization 33

Chapter 4: Affirmations (Thought, Feeling And Belief) 45

Chapter 5: Actions 57

Chapter 6: Being A Deliberate Creator 75

Chapter 7: The Law Of Resonance 83

Chapter 8: Lulls, Doubts and Resistance 97

Chapter 9: Tools Of The Trade 107

Chapter 10: Ancient Secrets of Magic 121

Chapter 11: Summary and Conclusion 129

Links Page 137

Exciting Video Course Offer 139

Introduction

Greetings! I am so happy and grateful that you chose to read my book. I am also excited to go on this journey of discovery with you. My goal when initially outlining this book was to make it unique compared to the other Law of Attraction books I have read. I mean I really wanted to bust out the absolute coolest, most useful Law of Attraction book ever. With such a lofty goal for a book on such a popular subject I knew I had to identify, then tap into, the aspect of the Law of Attraction that I was most passionate about. As I was thinking about pure passion I recalled an interview I saw once with the unprecedented eleven-time world champion of surfing Kelly Slater.

I grew up in Florida near Sebastian and Kelly used to surf at Sebastian Inlet when he was a kid. Back then he was obviously talented, but there were a few other kids his age who were basically as good as he was at the time.

I always wondered what made him so exceedingly successful compared to those other kids. Then I saw a video where someone asked him (after he had won several world surfing titles) what his favorite thing in the world to do was. What he said was, "go surfing." Not win contests, get trophies or be on magazine covers. The person asking the question kind of laughed as if the answer were too obvious, then asked, "Okay, what's your *second* most favorite thing to do?" Kelly instantly said, "talk about surfing."

It is that same type of instinctual consuming passion that I feel about the Law of Attraction. But even though Kelly Slater likes to talk about surfing, compete and win contests, and explore the world searching for perfect waves what he really loves to do most is actually surf. I enjoy reading about the Law of Attraction. I also like to talk about it with my friends and I do love writing about it. But what I love to do most is *apply* the Law of Attraction and watch it come to life and just plain work. With that thought I knew I had the essence of this book. I decided to put all of my passion for applying the Law of Attraction into creating something special for people ready for exactly such a book. I wrote this book for one reason: *So you can fully understand and absolutely apply the Law of Attraction to accomplish your most treasured desires.*

Introduction

I have consciously included aspects of the Law of Attraction that seem to be left out of many other books in the genre. Such as some crafty ways to visualize beyond just picturing your goal, and ways to deal with people who have no belief in your vision. In these pages we will also explore what to do about the lulls, doubts and resistance we all eventually encounter on the journey toward our highest goals and endeavors. However, as someone who understands the Law of Attraction, in this book I never give more attention to these issues than to their elegant and valuable solutions. Any such potential pitfalls along the path of the Law of Attraction are given only the minimal attention it takes to nimbly step over them.

In the months I have spent writing this book, it just so happens that I have accomplished some of my most treasured long-term intentions and goals. In doing so, I have drawn upon my own direct experience and interpretation of the Law of Attraction as I researched, outlined and crafted this work. Doing so has been an incredible trip.

My first published book was Espresso For Your Goals, which combined a methodical system of goal setting with the Law of Attraction. It was and is a huge success. That book rose to number two on Amazon's Bestseller list in the Self-Help / Motivational category during the book's free promotion and found its way into the hands of over

1,770 readers. But that book was written as a short, down and dirty how-to blueprint for high achievers who need a concentrated energy boost for their goal setting life.

This book is more of a flowing narrative and is for Law of Attraction fans who need a second wind for their Deliberate Creation adventures. This Law of Attraction book is valuable for one simple fact:

This book is focused on *applying the Law of Attraction*.

Since the Law of Attraction is a natural law, just like gravity or inertia, it has rules and guiding principles. I have used those guiding principles to write a concise, easy to follow book to help people actually *apply* the Law of Attraction. Applying the Law of Attraction can be a tricky subject to try to convey in a book. Doing exactly that to the best of my ability has been the most challenging thing I have ever attempted as a writer. It has also been the most exciting experience you can imagine. Writing about the Law of Attraction is a seductive project for any motivational writer, because the real application of the phenomenon has such powerful potential to literally *change people's lives* as the cliché goes. One of my strengths is the impulse to convey complex subjects in simple ways. I poured every ounce of my effort and energy into applying that strength in order to create a book of pure, useful value.

That being the case I have opted for a direct, straight-forward approach. In short, here is how we are going to do this. In the chapters that follow we will first dive into the Law of Attraction as a paradigm shift in the way we look at the world of getting stuff done. Then we will explore what I have defined as the four stages of Deliberate Creation: Destination, Visualization, Affirmations, and Actions. Each of these stages will be explored and mapped out in its own chapter, so you can get a firm grasp on the territory and go on to achieve your highest intentions. Those chapters are the preparation, tools and provisions for your journey.

Then there is a chapter on being a Deliberate Creator, which gives us an experiment to put those stages into play with a real-life project. After that there are sections for understanding resonance (or aligning vibration), and dealing with lulls, doubts and resistance. Then I will give you some of my favorite advanced tools to use as you apply the Law of Attraction in your life. Finally, as sort of a fun bonus, I included a chapter on the Ancient Secrets Of Magic, where we will explore some esoteric knowledge that just so happens to align perfectly with our most modern ideas of scientific accomplishment.

Then we'll wrap it up with the Summary and Conclusion. I have also included a Links Page so you will have all of the valuable links mentioned throughout the book gathered in one convenient place. Finally, at the very end, there is a cool Video Course Offer that is such a huge hit that I decided to include it in this book as well.

My intention when setting out to create this work was to deliver results on the subject of actually navigating the Law of Attraction. I wanted the book to be exceedingly valuable as well as fun to read. If you are reading these words, then you have attracted this book into your experience. Applying the Law of Attraction can be the most rewarding adventure imaginable. I hope that within these pages, you find the preparation, tools and provisions you need for a successful and thrilling journey. If you are ready to consciously and deliberately apply the powerful Law of Attraction, come with me and let's do it together. This will be a rocking good time. Let's go!

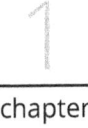
chapter

A Paradigm Shift

There is something interesting that happens when a truth that was previously understood by a mere few, becomes widespread knowledge. In our popular language we call this a *paradigm shift*.

One classic example of a paradigm shift was that moment when it became widely understood that the Earth was actually round (or a sphere) as opposed to flat. Up until that point I would guess that most people had never really given it much thought. The overall terrain looked flat, everyone agreed and that was that. It did not directly affect their lives and they had bigger issues to worry about.

However, once it was proposed otherwise, I'm sure there were arguments, discussions and scientific experiments and eventually it became the consensus that the

Earth was indeed round. Isn't it fascinating that once a new paradigm is accepted, we all just agree and move on? While there may still be a Flat Earth Society, the general population lives and acts as if the Earth were round and so far, so good. All of us alive today were born into this Round Earth age and we (just like the Flat Earth dwellers of a few hundred years ago) rarely question the status of the planet's shape. Just like our ancestors of Flat Earth, we have bigger fish to fry.

There are a few paradigm concepts, however, that do creep into our everyday discussions with direct impact on the decisions and results in our lives. One such concept is the economic model of scarcity versus abundance. The older, traditional western model of economics (and the one taught when I was a university student) is one of lack. That economic model proposes that wants and needs are *unlimited* and resources are *limited*. The science of *economics* is to allocate these *limited resources* to satisfy the *unlimited demand*. To me that mission sounds like it would be destined to fail by definition.

The new, more organic understanding of resources and demand is cyclical. Resources flow through a cycle of consumption and reallocation. And even in the strictest example of scarcity (such as a village of five hundred people with one well that only provides enough water for four hundred people) the cyclical process still applies. The village either finds more water by importing it or digging a new well, or decreases in population as people move away or die of thirst. Now I'm not saying that people dying of thirst is an ideal situation, but the fact is that looking at the same situation from a western economic policy of trying to satisfy five hundred people's thirst with a four hundred person supply of water would not save a single soul. The economist in charge would still have to dig a well, import some water or move. As soon as he took any of those actions he would find himself in the organic cycle of either tapping into a greater supply or reallocating his own demand to a more hydrated location. So are wants and needs unlimited beyond all supply, or does supply and demand flow in a cycle? A quick story will illustrate the two opposing viewpoints.

Once I was having a chat with a coworker about the weekend ahead and I mentioned that my landscaped yard was dry and that I planned to set up a big tower sprinkler I had made to water the plants. (Tropical landscaping is a hobby of mine.) This coworker remarked, half-jokingly, "Oh, so you are one of those people who wastes all the water."

My reply was, "Well, not really. Because the water just goes into the plants and the ground, and the air and it all returns into the water cycle and becomes ground water and rain and so you really never waste water unless you pollute it."

The lady just kind of looked at me and said something like, "You're weird," and walked off.

She could be right but the story illustrates two opposing economic paradigms. Hers is one of lack. Demand for water must be unlimited, and since water comes in bottles from the store, or through pipes from the water company, it must be from a finite supply. If you water your yard with it, that water is obviously not going back into the bottles in the store, so you must be using it up, or wasting it.

My viewpoint comes from a deeper understanding that water is a part of the Earth and continually cycles from lakes that feed rivers, which flow into oceans, that evaporate into clouds which eventually create rains that fill lakes again and so on.

Consider how such a viewpoint could affect people's relationship with money. One person continually laments that there is just never enough money to go around. However, I have read that if we divided up all of the money in the world evenly, there would be enough for every single person alive to have over a million dollars. Now, dividing that money and distributing it is a job for the free market and not socialist or communist politicians. However, it is similar to the water cycle analogy. If you think lack, you

A Paradigm Shift

see lack and you, well, lack. If you realize the greater truth that there is more than enough and that it all flows in a cycle, then you understand that something like money, is just a representation of value. The more value you add, the more money you earn from the millions of dollars flowing through the system.

All of this discussion is necessary because it clearly illustrates the paradigm shift that this chapter is about. That shift is away from the idea that we live in a cold, material Universe and that we hatched into it by some lucky accident to cling to our lifeless rock until we die and fall off. Our paradigm is shifting toward one where we recognize the Universe as being completely alive and that we are not only alive in it, but that our life actually *is* the life of the Universe. Just as the living cells in your body are what make you alive, so we are the cells of the planet and the galaxies.

What does this have to do with the Law of Attraction? Well, there can be no Law of Attraction in a lifeless, nonresponsive Universe. The energy of communication must be reciprocal for any exchange to occur.

Whether this is your first book on the Law of Attraction, or one of many that you have read, you have still been born into a time when this concept (that your thoughts become the events and circumstances of your life) is only now becoming a widespread topic of discussion.

Have wise people always known this? Yes. Does everyone accept and live by it now? Not yet. But that will not stop you from applying it. You see the question is not whether the Law of Attraction is valid or not. The question is will you choose to consciously manage it in your day-to-day life? My guess is that to do so is your intention, and that is the reason you are reading this book. If you have ever experienced a deliberate intention manifest into your experience then you know the excitement of applying this law, and this book will help you refine and improve the process. If you have only read about it and are ready to see it work, then this book is going to be really fun and valuable for you as well. Welcome to the coolest paradigm shift since the Earth became round!

The foremost Law of Attraction rule, then, (and it's a big one) is that the Law of Attraction represents a paradigm shift in our culture resulting from the understanding that the Universe is alive, intelligent, and active and that we are a living part of it.

The main principle for applying a paradigm shift is to accept it. The Universe is alive and you are a living part of it. As such, you are connected to all things as surely as every molecule of every plant is connected to the air in the atmosphere, the Sun and all points beyond. To prove this beyond any doubt I offer you this simple analogy.

Consider the organs in your body. We typically

imagine them to be separate things. However, a simple question reveals their interconnected nature. Which is more important, your lungs, your heart or your brain? The answer is that all are equally critical. Remove any single one and the others would die along with the entire person. The Universe is exactly the same. Which is more important to life on Earth, the plants, the Earth's atmosphere, or the Sun? The answer is the same: each one is critical. Remove the Sun, and watch how fast the plants on Earth vanish. Remove the plants and gasp as the atmosphere fades. Delete the Atmosphere and it's "See ya later suckers," to all life as we know it around here. To illustrate the idea even further, consider a plant such as a banana tree. We think of it as being separate from the air, but in reality air flows through it as the banana tree inhales carbon dioxide and exhales oxygen. The tree looks different from the air, but it is not separated from it. In the same way all things are connected. From the plants and animals of Earth all the way to the deepest reaches of the cosmos.

"Walk with me through the Universe. And along the way see how all of us are connected. Feast the eyes of your soul on the Love that abounds, in all places at once, seemingly endless, like your own existence."

— **Stephen Hawking**

It's not only the physical components of our Universe that are interdependent and connected as constituents of a greater whole. Our own individual thoughts, actions and accomplishments are also connected parts of the universal flowing life. In fact, the word *Universe* means *one song*.

Consider that the most cutting-edge science has concluded that all things are variations of vibration, or in other words, energy. The sounds of music, or the very song that our Universe is named for are nothing more than tones of vibration that we can hear. In the same way, so too is every physical object nothing more than particles vibrating or oscillating at various frequencies in what amounts to mostly empty space. This is initially hard to understand because some physical objects just seem so hard. Think of it like this. A fan blade is spinning. If it is barely spinning you can stick your finger between the blades if you are fast enough. However, once the fan blade increases to a fast enough speed, the disc it creates is virtually solid. If you try to stick your finger through that spinning disc (even though the spaces between the blades are still there) you will injure your finger, just like you might hurt your foot if you kick a *solid* rock.

The fact is that there are spaces between the atoms of the rock as well, but the tiny particles that make up the rock's atoms are spinning at such an incredible speed

A Paradigm Shift

(the speed of light it has been proposed and measured) that for all practical purposes the rock is solid. The only reason it makes any difference at all is because it is important to understand that this entire connected Universe is all made up of vibration, or energy. Why is this such a big deal? Because your thoughts and feelings are nothing more than energy as well. The Law of Attraction functions because of resonance, whereby like frequencies stimulate and respond to each other. This is another way to say like attracts like. There is truly only your thought, and all of its dazzling reflections.

When your thoughts, intentions and actions are in alignment with your highest goals and visions, the Universe will respond to the frequency of that vibration. Unseen doors will open, resources will arrive and your experience will reflect the thoughts that most frequently populate your mind. It works for everyone. It works all of the time. It never fails. That is why we call it the *Law* of Attraction. If you still wonder whether or not such a law exists, then honestly and objectively consider your overall way of thinking over the last year about one specific subject.

Your current reality is a reflection of your persistent thoughts over time. If you have suffered some tragedy that was not your fault, then I fully sympathize with you. In this mortal life people get hurt and sad things happen.

In my life I have suffered exceedingly unjust loss. The fact is, however, that every life or love I have lost is no more dead or gone than every person ever born is or will be someday. The searing, acute understanding that those difficult experiences imposed upon me was the understanding of gratefulness, not bitterness.

With every breath in, I inhale this abundant life. With every breath out, I exhale the thought *thank you*. With every step I take, I take a step toward my goals. And with every word I speak, I try to express encouragement, compassion and consideration. These attitudes are not in spite of the tragic painful losses in my life; they are because of them.

So regardless of what you have been through (regardless of what you have or have not accomplished in your life so far) your predominant thoughts have either directly caused your situation, or precisely decorated your interpretation of it. Understand that all parts of the living Universe are connected variations of living vibration. Viewing the Universe as a vast, mutual connection that includes your own thoughts is a paradigm shift away from the Newtonian Universe of inanimate billiard balls clicking about.

So that is a pretty heavy rule to start the book out with, especially when we are talking about applying these rules. But really applying this rule is the easiest part of the Law of Attraction. All you need to do is simply realize that all things are connected at a fundamental level. Yes, good guys and bad guys. Thugs, pimps, pushers and saints. Does that mean they are the same? No. But it does mean they are all part of the same system. Therefore (and here is the *"applying the Law of Attraction"* part) they each create their own experiences by virtue of the predominant thoughts they continually hold in their mind.

The questions that those who argue against the Law of Attraction always seem to invoke are often focused on victim scenarios. Questions like, "Well, Mr. Smarty-pants. Are you telling me that the victim of a mugging (or any other tragedy) created that event with their thoughts?"

The answer to that question is **no**. And the reason things like that happen is because we do live in a consensus reality where people can take actions (based on their thoughts) and those actions can sometimes affect others, for good or ill. That is the nature of a material physical life.

My classic response to that victim remark is this: don't let the things you can't control keep you from acting towards those things you can control.

You can't influence the thoughts and actions of others very much. You can, however, control your own thoughts and actions. Those who do so consciously are the highest achievers in the world. Does that mean nothing bad ever happens to them? Of course not. But to use the fact that sometimes crappy things happen to people, as an excuse to keep yourself and others from living a deliberate, creative life, is to play into the hands of those who would control you through fear.

Realize that the Law of Attraction represents a paradigm shift toward a view of the entire Universe as interconnected, mutually responsive energy. Choose your thoughts and choose your reality. But still look both ways before crossing the street. And if you are able to stop someone from hurting someone else, or of it is your job to bring criminals to justice, then do so with Godspeed and with the gratefulness of everyone you help and protect, whether they ever realize it or not.

chapter 2

Destination
(Ideal Desired Result)

In the broadest sense the Law of Attraction gives you more of what you focus your attention on. Many have said that the Law of Attraction gives you what you want. That isn't necessarily true. It equates your experience toward that which you give the majority of your thoughts and feelings. Therefore, the first stage in applying the Law of Attraction is to clearly define a Destination (or ideal desired result) so that you have a thought worthy of your attention.

Even the most confident among us will sometimes awake suddenly in the night to an acute thought of pure fear. Exactly that happened to me once when I was a mere two days away from my last day working the corporate management job I had held for the previous seven years and three months. Prior to that I had held a similar job with another large company for three or four years. A management job with a tiny business was my role before that and prior to that I had either been in college or the few wrong jobs I had between the two.

Now, in two days, I was going to be completely self-employed as a writer and internet publisher. The reality of it had been clearly identified by my deep subconscious as I slept, and I guess it decided to text message my conscious mind at three a.m. and we all jumped up in bed together and the question that both parts of my mind had for my ego was, "Are you crazy?"

You are walking away from a guaranteed salary which is well more than you need in the middle of the highest unemployment the nation has known since your grandmother was a kid in the depression and had to make her own toys out of buttons and string!

But the reality was, that salary was the only thing I would be walking away from. Yes I had loved that job. In fact, someone once asked me (near the end of my career there) what my favorite job ever had been. My answer without hesitation was, "This job five years ago." It's no secret that I was a manager for Starbucks Coffee Company for over seven years. Now here I was leaving to write full time and I was faced with having to buy my own health insurance and my own coffee. The most frightening thing was I wasn't sure if I would ever be able to afford the coffee!

But I acted on faith in myself as a writer and as someone who has an ability to actualize, follow through, and create something from an idea. I had seen what I had been able to accomplish with the Law of Attraction up to that point and I knew if I could do those things then I could do anything. I made the decision to bow out gracefully and with the help of those I worked with was able to do just that in a way that was to the highest benefit of everyone involved. I would have expected nothing less from that outstanding organization, even if it had evolved into something quite different from the company I had signed on with nearly eight years before. I had planned everything out, but the thought of not having a steady paycheck had awoken me at three a.m. and the fear was real.

In that moment I reminded myself of something basic. (Isn't it always the basics that we return to when the chips are down?) In the shortest description that basic principle was to always focus on my ideal desired result. That had gotten me through so many scary times before and I knew it wouldn't let me down in that moment. So I just repeated my number one goal a few times and went back to sleep. Instead of counting sheep, I repeated to myself, at first out loud and then dimming to an internal chant:

> "I am a published, professional, completely self-employed writer. I write for a living. I work for myself. I always have more money than I need."
>
> "I am a published, professional, completely self-employed writer. I write for a living. I work for myself. I always have more money than I need."
>
> "I am a published, professional, completely self-employed writer. I write for a living. I work for myself. I always have more money than I need."
>
> "I am a published, professional, completely self-employed writer. I write for a living. I work for myself. I always have more money than I...zzzzzzz."

The key to applying the power of your ideal desired result is to understand that **what you give your attention to expands.** A great example of this is prohibition. Focus collective attention on stopping something, and watch the elaborate expansion of creativity that develops to perpetuate it. The classic argument for prohibiting some vice or victimless social behavior is that to *not* do so would, "send the wrong message." This is exactly an illustration of the concept that *the road to Hell is paved with good intentions.*

Destination (Ideal Desired Result)

In such a situation, the intended message becomes more important to some than the actual result or outcome. The war on drugs, for instance, creates more refined and destructive drugs, a subculture of crime and a general distrust of authority while having very little actual success in stopping drug use or traffic. This situation mirrors the prohibition of alcohol from over eighty years ago. The more collective and institutionalized attention we, as a society, give to the *drug problem* the more of a *drug problem* we get. Anyone who suggests stopping the so-called *war on drugs* is immediately marginalized as someone who *"must want illegal drugs available in elementary school vending machines!"* That kind of irrational reactionary defense of an ineffective policy is exactly illustrative of the inevitable, logical direction toward which focusing on a problem will take your thoughts. Now, in this hypothetical example, we have a person so passionate about stopping drugs, that they have creatively had and voiced the thought of hard-drug vending machines for school kids. To what end will that type of drama mongering take you?

Here is the cool part about the Law of Attraction with regard to the fact that *what you give your attention to expands*. Once you realize and understand this rule, you can simply choose what to give your attention to.

The guiding principle for applying this Destination

stage is to first clearly define, then focus the majority of your thoughts upon, your ideal desired result (as opposed to its opposite). In other words, to proactively apply the Law of Attraction

> ***simply (but always) give the majority***
> ***of your attention to your Destination***
> ***(your ideal desired result).***

This is the reason that vision boards are so powerful, because you skip the "hows" and the "what if I don'ts" and go straight to the feeling of your completed goal. (But more on Visualization in that chapter.)

When you are trying to manifest a specific goal, then the first thing you should do is clearly define your ideal desired result. State your intention in the present, as if it were completed and infuse it with emotion and gratitude. This will give you something to focus on. An example would be, *"I am so happy and grateful now that I earn a solid $4000 per month or more with my pool cleaning business!"*

Then, on that day when you start to worry that your pool cleaning business isn't exactly raking it in, remember to focus your mind on that intention or goal. Really stop and repeat to yourself, *"I am so happy and grateful now that I earn a solid $4000. per month or more with my pool cleaning business!"* Believe a way will come then take whatever action you can think of to move in the direction of your goal. Or when that clear potential action jumps into your face, take it.

Is it okay to identify or express a current problem or bad situation? Yes, in fact it is paramount for survival. However, if it's your intention to do something about it, only consider it for long enough to clearly define your desire for something better, then focus on that moving forward. In the LOA community, we call this identifying contrast. Look at it in the same way as accidently touching a hot stove. When you realize the stove is hot you pull your hand away. You don't hold your hand there while it smolders and have long drawn out conversations about the temperature of the stove or how badly it hurts. When you identify contrast, immediately choose your desired Destination then move toward that with your thoughts instead.

At this point there is something to be cautious of when you are on your way to achieving a goal or intention. You may have clearly identified your ideal desired result and given tons of thought to it so far. But then, as time passes, it is natural to begin to casually wonder where your manifestation is. When will you gain some ground here? These are subtle variations of *what you don't want*. In other words, they are the opposite of your ideal desired result, clothed in the disguises of what you do want. They have cleverly inserted your Destination into your thoughts, but with the sneaky attachment of *when* or *why not yet?* When those types of questions or doubts begin to arise, just displace them with thoughts of your goal achieved.

You may be familiar with my Theory of Displacement if you have read my previous book, Espresso For Your Goals. In short, the Theory of Displacement asserts that rather than trying to identify and banish your negative, limiting beliefs, you can simply wash them away by continually focusing on positive, affirming beliefs instead.

"Fill your mind up with the things that you want, until they overflow all the things that you don't"

The Theory of Displacement is of particular importance when you are trying to focus more thoughts on your ideal desired result for one simple but powerful reason: doubt and certainty cannot occupy the same thought. Continually replace thoughts of failure with phrases such as these:

"Yes this is possible."

"I'll figure it out."

"I always have more money than I need."

"I can do this. Others have succeeded at this. So will I."

In addition to those times when you start to casually wonder when your goal will be accomplished, there is another, more drastic situation that requires you to be cautious and mindful when applying the Law of Attraction. It is the moment of severe contrast. Severe contrast is that moment of sheer anger or frustration concerning a current undesirable circumstance. You can clearly identify it when you hear yourself say things like, *"I can't believe I have to deal with this right now."* Or, in the more succinct parlance of our times, *"This sucks!"*

Having a moment when you feel pure disgust about something you either lack, or wish you didn't have to do, and identifying what you actually **do** want is the same thing. They are just two sides of the same coin. Not like a fork in the road with two possible angles, but like a single long, straight road you find yourself on and you can either go north or south. You see it is the same road. It just simultaneously has the possibility to take you in two opposite directions. The direction you go in (and therefore the destination at which you will inevitably arrive) depends on the thought you choose to follow.

Follow the thought of contrast (what you don't have

or what you don't want) and you will go down the road toward more of that. Use those moments of heavy contrast to stop and say, *"Hey, wait a minute here. Toward more of **that** is not the direction I want to go in."* Then turn around and move in the opposite direction with thoughts of what you would rather have and experience.

Recognize that what you give your attention to expands. Then proactively apply this rule to your life by focusing more of your thoughts on your ideal desired result.

chapter 3

Visualization

The second stage of applying the Law of Attraction is using Visualization to build belief. Visualization is just a fancy word for daydreaming. That is, vividly imagining a state or event. I would bet that most people initially discover this ability sometime in elementary school. Let's go back to those days for just a minute.

* * *

Imagine that you are sitting in your classroom. The teacher is going on and on, but you would much rather be riding your bike around the neighborhood. All of a sudden you can picture yourself on the bike and you feel the handlebar grips in your hands. You stand to peddle and feel the rush of passing air. You hear the blackbirds chatter on the wire above as you sail under them and they cheer you on. The neighbor dog comes out to bark and run along with you like he always does until he reaches the end of his block where he stops and heads back home. He's a good dog. Now you have enough speed to coast and swerve so you sit back on the seat and lift your feet from the peddles and lean back some and…

"Mr. Goodrich! Would you care to join the rest of us? We are learning about fractions today and this is very important."

* * *

Back to reality. In the public school system, kids who are good at visualizing are quickly labeled as daydreamers who don't pay attention. In fact, historically, visualization has been generally discouraged from childhood right through into adulthood. This type of pretending is viewed as *not being realistic*, and that is most certainly true. There is a time to be realistic. However, if we as individuals or a society are ever going to accomplish anything *new* then we must learn to visualize effectively.

If certain people had never been *unrealistic* and visualized beyond their current reality we would still be without the wheel, automobiles, airplanes, electricity, cellphones, computers, and worst of all we would not have eBooks! (The horror.)

So throughout history people have used visualization

Visualization

to accomplish great things. Yes they had to take action. Yes they had to actually *do* stuff. But it is always the thought and the vision which precedes any accomplishment. Alchemists, mystics, spiritual teachers, scientists and philosophy professors alike have expressed this idea throughout the ages. From the Bible which states that *"As a man thinketh in his heart, so is he,"* to Einstein who remarked that, *"Imagination is more important than knowledge."*

Once you have your Destination clearly defined, it is the Visualization stage that fuels the Law of Attraction. You may not be planning to invent the next world-changing product but you will still have to master visualization if you intend to use the Law of Attraction to accomplish or gain something that is not a part of your current experience.

Mastering visualization sounds harder than it is. It is actually easy and fun. It's just like pretending to ride your bike as you sit in class. You get to skip *how*, and *by when* and all of those thoughts that stop people from trying. You get to go, in your mind, straight to the day of your goal accomplished.

The guiding principle for applying this stage is to ***proactively use Visualization to mentally experience your goal as achieved.*** In other words simply imagine yourself in a situation where your intention is a reality for a few minutes each day. This is not something that should take up vast amounts of your time. You only need to actively visualize any one goal for five minutes or so per day. If you are new to visualizing, you may spend some time getting the hang of it, but put that time in. Doing this is one of the most powerful exercises that you will ever engage in. Do not be discouraged if your goal is not at your feet the next day after your first try. This takes time, just like growing a plant from a seed takes time.

I bet you have visualized to some degree many times before. Have you ever looked at the pictures of a resort before going on vacation? You can picture yourself in the beautiful room, seated in the trendy café or relaxing at the beachside tiki bar as Isaac makes you a pina colada. The only difference between doing that and visualizing to apply the Law of Attraction, is that when proactively visualizing for the Law of Attraction, you choose the pictures and situations of your goals achieved.

Maybe it's your goal to sell your home and you picture yourself helping the realtor affix the *Sold* sticker across the *For Sale* sign in your yard. Perhaps your goal is to pass the Bar Exam or get accepted to your favorite University and you picture yourself opening the letter that contains the good news (*Congratulations, we are pleased to inform you that…*). Visualization works very well when you imagine scenarios like these that would naturally take place after your goal is accomplished. Also it doesn't always have to be done by sitting quietly in a darkened room (although that does work). You can also do more spontaneous things that don't take up any extra time from your day at all. For example, if one of your goals is to have a major literary agent represent your book series to be published by a big publishing house, you could pretend to make a phone call as you eat your lunch in the park.

"Hello Sandra! This is Les. I just wanted to let you know that I just signed all of the contract pages for the next book and everything looks great. I sent back your copies so just let me know if you need anything else. Yes. Oh yes, I'd be happy to do that interview for Writers Digest anytime. Okay great. Just have them call me. Awesome. Thank you and I'll see you at the annual Exceedingly Successful and Nauseatingly Happy Novelists Convention in New York next month! Ciao!"

Let your imagination and creativity run wild when you visualize. Have fun with this. It's the emotions of having it now that you are after. The more fun you have and the more excitement you can feel in the process, the better. As you progress from initial idea to completed reality you will undoubtedly encounter moments when you wonder if anything is happening. *Where are the opportunities? Where is the help?*

This is normal because you are just on your way to your goal. Don't stop. Keep going. This is the spot where a belief that *this doesn't work* will try to creep in. Do not cross the line of giving more of your thought and belief to the fiction that the Law of Attraction does not work. If you do that, then the Law of Attraction will prove to you that the Law of Attraction does not work by giving you exactly what you think about the most. Get it? The Law of Attraction is not biased. It does not care if you believe in it or not. It simply always gives you what you focus on with the majority of your thoughts and beliefs (which in turn determine your actions) and thus your reality.

One of my favorite analogies is that of a road trip. I always use the example of driving to the Florida Keys, because I live on the coast in South Florida and I love to drive down to the Keys to dive for lobster in the summer. It's one of the most amazing drives in the country and it never gets old. From where I live it takes about six hours and Miami is halfway. I never get to Miami and say, "Hey, this isn't the Keys! We have been driving for hours and we haven't seen the Keys yet. I guess the Keys trip was just a fool's errand and trying to get there was a useless dream. Let's go back home."

The reason I would never say that is because I *know* how long it should take to get to the Keys. I have driven there twenty times or more and I recognize the landmarks along the way. When I get through Florida City and see the Everglades stretch from the roadside to the horizon, I know I will be seeing bright green water soon. Catching that first glimpse of the emerald-colored Atlantic is a thrill every time.

However, when we are setting out to accomplish a grand goal or new intention in our life, the road toward it can seem much less certain. Things arise and we wonder if this is the end. Perhaps our plans must be adapted and often we simply don't get to our destination as quickly as we had imagined we might. These moments of doubt or recognition of your goal unfulfilled are the times known as contrast. When experiencing contrast, visualization is your ticket to do two critical things.

First, visualization is what fuels the Law of Attraction because this is how you give attention to, think about and create the feelings of a state of being that is not yet real. Visualization is your pathway to skip beyond your current circumstance and go directly (in your mind) to your intended outcome. Will visualization alone cause all of your dreams to come true? No. Writers who claim it will have probably caused many rational people to dismiss the Law of Attraction without any further investigation.

The fact is, though, that visualization is an indispensable step in the process.

Secondly visualization helps build your belief. You believe you can do something, because you have practiced it in your mind. That belief causes the same (or better) muscle memory as physical practice. This phenomenon has been documented in many cases. Perhaps one of the most famous is the Visual Motor Rehearsal program instituted by Dr. Dennis Waitley for the USA Olympic teams in the 1980's and 1990's.

One tool to help you visualize (and one that has received a fair amount of attention) is a vision board. A vision board is a tool that you create and populate with pictures, phrases and goal statements. A well-aligned vision board facilitates the focus of your thoughts. The vision board is the Deliberate Creator's navigational chart. It is exactly like an explorer's map. Is a sailor's coastal chart the territory? No. But it is an indispensable tool for reaching a destination nonetheless. Vision boards are effective because they allow you to bypass how, and take your thoughts straight to the end result. You can focus on a picture of a boat you want and imagine yourself at the helm. As you do this you are fantasizing about being in the boat, riding across the water with the wind in your face and the purr of the engine behind you. As you are on this boat ride in your imagination, you are probably not picturing yourself reading from a windblown, damp outline of questions for your bank loan officer, who hangs on as you bounce over waves, his tie flying in the breeze. You are simply conjuring the feelings of having the dang boat already. It is that feeling and those thoughts of having it already that will draw you into the actions and circumstances that make owning the boat a reality.

You are matching the feeling of your current moment with the feeling of having your goal fulfilled. Consciously doing that takes advantage of the understanding that all of the diversity in the Universe is actually just varying vibrations. This is often referred to as managing the law of resonance. The law of resonance could also be called the law of matching vibrations. Strike a tuning fork in a room full of tuning forks and the other forks in the room with the same frequency (or in the same key) will begin to vibrate also. This is the same reason that a radio station can vibrate a wire at a certain frequency and your radio can hear their broadcast when you tune your antenna to vibrate at that same rate. Consider what you wish to be, do, or have, then consciously and more often give your thoughts and feelings to the frequency (or feeling) of it as already done. Whatever you think about and feel about the most is what you will experience in your life. But you have to believe that you can do it first.

Some might say, *"Why don't I just get in the car, drive*

to the yacht broker and buy the boat?" Well, if you believe you can do that and you have the resources then do it. In that case you would not need to visualize much. You would not need a vision board and you would simply be talking about a purchase. At the same time, if every time you see a nice big boat you say (to yourself or someone else), "That must be nice," and you think and feel deeply that you will never have a boat like that, then you never will. Guaranteed.

However, visualization is a tool to help you build belief and find resources when you are setting out to do something that no one would think you could do or that requires a heroic effort for even you to believe. Visualization is for taking large steps in goal accomplishment. Remember, a vision board alone will accomplish nothing. But creating a vision board of pictures and phrases that match your ideal desired results, then focusing on it with a clear mind for a few minutes each day, and vividly imagining your highest goals as reality for five minutes each, can honestly move mountains.

You can spend money buying vision board kits from famous Law of Attraction writers and some of them are outstanding. But you can also make your own and get just as many results from it. The one I use is on a roll-up scroll calendar that I got for free from a Chinese take-out restaurant. It is plastic and made to look like bamboo and has a golden string on top that you can hang it from. I just covered it with poster board cut to size so I could tape pictures and put sticky notes on it. I have my Main Mission, Top 4 Goals, and Top 4 Visions on sticky notes in rows, and between the rows I have pictures of some of my goals and visions. I like it because since it is made to hang from the string I can take it from room to room, or hang it out of sight on the back of a door when I'm not using it. On the back of it I have also put a note that says "Success Board" and when I achieve something I have been working on, I move the sticky note to the "Success Board" side. Every so often I will look at that side as well, to remind myself of what can be achieved, particularly when I am having a moment of heavy contrast where my goals seem overdue.

Remember to keep your written goals, your affirmations and your vision board notes and images in alignment. Alignment is what builds momentum with your thoughts. If you update or refine one of your Top 4 Goals, immediately update that goal's note on your vision board. This does two things. It adds conviction and faith to your belief in the power of your own goal setting tools, and it creates a unified direction so your thoughts move toward consistent ideal desired results.

chapter 4

Affirmations
(Thought, Feeling And Belief)

When pilots describe a plane's orientation to the horizon they use three basic terms: pitch, roll and yaw. In layman's terms pitch is the angle up or down of the nose, roll is the angle up or down of the wings, and yaw is the angle of the body of the craft to the left or right. Collectively these three angles of flight dynamics are known as the plane's *attitude*. So in a literal sense, it's a plane's *attitude* that determines the direction it will go.

For people this is true as well. It is our attitude that determines the direction and circumstances of our lives.

The Merriam-Webster Dictionary defines attitude as *a mental position, feeling or emotion with regard to a fact or state*. So it is the *position* or *feeling* that you take concerning something or someone in your life. Sometimes our attitudes can be exactly correct, and these instances serve us well. Imagine that you regard a certain acquaintance as untrustworthy because you have verified proof of their inclination to habitually lie. If they tell you that one of your best friends was slandering your good name at the cocktail party you recently missed, you would be wise to respectfully approach your friend about the incident rather than burst into their office calling them a back-stabbing traitor. In such a case your attitude about your lying acquaintance (even though it could be considered a negative attitude) would be one that would most likely help you.

Now consider another situation. You receive your electric bill and it is higher than the previous month. You immediately exclaim that, *"Everything is so expensive. It's no wonder that I'm broke all the time!"* The fact is that if you continually affirm that to yourself, you will only perpetuate it. If you are constantly saying *I'm broke all the time* then that is your attitude toward money. If you are one of those people who catch yourself saying that or something like it, you probably even defend the attitude by saying *"Yeah but it's true!"*

Okay, so it's true. But ask yourself this: where has talking about it all the time gotten you? Has beating that drum brought more money to you? No. And it never will.

Affirmations (Thought, Feeling And Belief)

The fact is you simply cannot constantly say that you are broke, and then see the opportunities you might have to earn, save or create more money in your life. Just like a plane who's pitch is pointing down, can never fly up. It is a physical impossibility. But for some reason pessimistic people just love to argue against the Law of Attraction. Why? Because it's easier to blame others for their problems, than take responsibility for their own actions and results. But which of those two choices is more productive, rewarding and significant? Be careful here, because attitudes are built over years and lifetimes. Perhaps you have heard yourself or someone you know say something like this before:

> *"Well, just **saying** that I have more money isn't going to **get** me more money."*

That is true. Just saying that you have more money is not going to get you more money. Exactly like *just sitting in a car* is not going to *get you to the movie theater*, but it is the undisputed first step.

So to apply the Law of Attraction you must be mindful of your attitude toward the things you wish to change and improve. Begin to shift your attitude by shifting the thoughts and the phrases you repeat to yourself about those subjects. Create a series of phrases that come from the attitude of your goal accomplished. If it's more money that you want, start saying to yourself, *"I always have an abundance of money,"* even if it isn't true yet. (Especially if it isn't true yet.) Why? Because it's like going to the movie theater: you have to get in the car first. You would never say, *"Well we obviously aren't at the movie theater, and that was our goal, so there is no use wasting our time getting into that stupid car. The car is just in the driveway and we didn't want to go to the driveway! The Law of Attraction doesn't work."*

Now I know that extreme analogy may sound preposterous, but that is exactly the kind of logic that stops so many people from starting down the road to proactively managing the incredible Law of Attraction in their lives.

These phrases, which describe an ideal desired result that you consciously begin to repeat, are known as affirmations. The fact is, we all use affirmations whether we do so consciously or not. (And they always work.) The phrase, *"I'm always broke,"* is an affirmation and look how deadly accurate and powerfully effective it is for so many people.

In my previous book, Espresso For Your Goals, I went into great depth defining and categorizing affirmations. In that book I divided affirmations into Pure

Affirmations (which are used to define goal states) and Refocus Affirmations (which are used to realign your thoughts when you experience severe contrast to your ideal situation).

When writing this book I have been very careful to not rehash the same material from Espresso For Your Goals especially since the two books both overlap on the subject of the Law of Attraction. However, that book is a down and dirty how-to blueprint for setting and working toward specific goals. This book is more philosophy and application of the general rules and attributes of the glorious Law of Attraction as a whole.

But when I came to this section on affirmations, I did draw upon Espresso For Your Goals for the content of the following three paragraphs. I think you would agree that doing so was the right thing.

> Affirmations are the Law of Attraction tribe's bread and butter. The highest performing athletes, salespeople and entrepreneurs use them. In general, affirmations are thoughts that you deliberately focus on in order to bring about change, or achieve something you never have before.

Affirmations are positive statements describing how you will feel and what you will experience when your ideal desired goals are achieved. The purpose of an affirmation is to build belief in a possibility when you set out to accomplish something you have never done before. Overall, they are thoughts that point toward what you desire. They are also useful for acknowledging current aspects of gratitude.

Affirmations are positive statements, set in the present, that describe your ideal desired result, or something you are grateful for. They are relatively short phrases that should be read or stated quickly. Affirmations are used to build habitual ways of thinking about a subject you wish to improve in your life. As such, they serve to program your subconscious mind. Affirmations are not designed to convince you that something is true if it isn't, but are simply a tool to fuel the Law of Attraction by filling your mind with more of what you want. Fill your mind up with the things that you want, until they overflow all of the things you don't.

Affirmations (Thought, Feeling And Belief)

Here are some examples of affirmations that I use everyday.

I always have an abundance of money.

I am Lucky. I am blessed. I expect and get miracles.

The Universe always sends me the opportunities, ideas, resources and relationships to smoothly accomplish my goals and visions.

I fully and deeply believe that I deserve the achievement of all of my goals.

Money flows to me with ease and in abundance.

My beliefs match my goals and visions.

My goals and dreams please me when I think about them.

I perform at an outstanding level and I earn abundant benefits by doing so.

My thoughts, feelings and actions are all aligned in the direction of my goals.

I go forth confidently giving thought and focus only to what I deserve.

I accomplish my goals everyday by my thoughts, feelings, beliefs and actions.

> Because my books are filled with value, they always sell remarkably well. The abundant income I earn from them is a reflection of the energy and effort that I put into them.
>
> I always take the Clear Actions needed to help manifest my visions. That's the fun part!
>
> I write and publish to give back to the world of books, that has given me so much throughout my life.

Use any of those affirmations that apply to you, and write your own for your personal goals and desires.

Remember that attitude is everything. It determines which way you go in life. One of the best ways to manage your attitude to your highest benefit is to use positive affirmations to guide your thoughts and feeling in the direction of your ideal desired results. Once you start to listen to yourself, you will quickly discover any negative affirmations that might be counterproductive. Consciously replace these habitual phrases with new thoughts that are in alignment with what you want, not with what you think is a problem or fault in the world.

Some say the Law of Attraction responds to your thoughts. Others insist it is your feelings that drive it. Still, there are those that claim that only your beliefs truly determine your point of attraction. The fact is all are

Affirmations (Thought, Feeling And Belief)

true. The Law of Attraction responds to your thoughts because thoughts influence feelings and beliefs, which in turn predicate your actions. Remember the analogy of your heart, lungs and brain of your body being interdependent like the Sun, air and water of the Earth? Well, thoughts, feelings, beliefs, actions and results share precisely that same interdependent nature. Does your heart keep you alive? Yes. Does your brain keep you alive? Yep. Both are critical just like your lungs. In the same way, the Law of Attraction functions from your thoughts, feelings, beliefs and actions. It is this connection, which clearly distinguishes the Law of Attraction from the power of positive thinking. Positive thinking is indispensible for achievement, but pure positive thinking often leaves out feelings, beliefs and actions.

It is your thoughts, feelings, beliefs and actions that the Law of Attraction responds to. In Law of Attraction lingo, these are the *vibration you offer*. The thing to understand is that sometimes a positive thought (or affirmation) can cause a negative feeling or belief (and therefore a negative vibration). If you find yourself struggling in a certain area, this may very well be what is happening.

For example, if your affirmation is "*I sold my house,*" yet every time you say it you hear the echo, *"No you haven't,"* then consider tweaking your affirmation. Simply adjust or refine your affirmation to a current truth but that also resonates at the same feeling of your intention or goal. This technique is what I have defined in the past as a Refocus Affirmation. Refocus Affirmations are true for you now, but equate to the same vibration or frequency as your ideal desired result. In the house-selling example you might refocus your affirmation to the phrase "*I love the thought of selling my house.*" That affirmation would be true, and it still makes you feel good to say it. You get no argument from the back of your mind and you are engaged in the feeling of having it now. You can also tie a refocus affirmation to something similar that you have done in the past. A phrase such as *"I loved the feeling of selling my townhouse a few years ago"* would be perfect, if you did sell your townhouse, and are now trying to sell a home. Use affirmations that help you feel great, no matter what the subject is. Align them with a positive attitude of confident expectations and you can achieve astounding results.

Also as a special bonus for buying my book, here is the website address to a private, unpublished, free affirmation video that I made for you:

http://youtu.be/s6A_1Uo6M18

It is twenty minutes of powerful affirmations and it's set to dreamy, relaxing music and features cool pictures. You can watch the pictures or just listen to the

Affirmations (Thought, Feeling And Belief)

affirmations in a relaxed state. Also I would suggest writing your own affirmations in the first person and recording yourself saying them using your smartphone or computer's audio recorder. Listening to affirmations is one of the most powerful Law of Attraction tools I have found. Listening to your own voice affirm with conviction takes this amazing tool over the top. Enjoy the free video and put the power of affirmations to work in your Law of Attraction arsenal.

chapter 5

Actions

So far we have covered understanding the Law of Attraction as a paradigm shift toward realizing the Universe as living, connected and supportive. We, as a part of that greater life, can and do align our thoughts with it when we draw into our experience those things and events that we focus on the most. As such, we have illustrated the importance of defining and giving more attention to our ideal desired results, rather than to our problems. We explored using the power of visualization to accomplish this and the impact that attitude and affirmation have on the process. Our time so far has been spent on these mental aspects of actively managing the Law of Attraction to our highest benefit.

In this chapter we will get into the next crucial step of applying the Law of Attraction and that is taking action. When I was at Florida State University I met a good friend who was also in the Entrepreneurship and Small Business Management program. He became somewhat of a mentor to me. He taught me many things about navigating a large organization (such as FSU) since he had made it through the Navy before arriving at the College of Business. One thing he always said was, "Never confuse activity with results."

The tools and theories I have outlined so far provide some pretty fertile ground for confusing activity with results, so be careful. Many newcomers to the Law of Attraction get into LOA theory, goal setting, visualization, repeating affirmations, and meditating on their vision boards and stay there forever. The reason is that doing all of that stuff really feels like taking action, and it is (to a point).

However you also have to take undisputed action steps toward your goals if you are ever going to move from activity to results. But if you are doing the other things with feeling and commitment, then the necessary actions will come easily. This should never be a struggle.

That does not mean that you will never have to do any work. People find out that I am a self-employed writer and internet publisher and often say things like, "Oh that must be nice. You never have to go to work."

Well I will confess that I rarely set an alarm clock

(but I do get up around seven a.m. every day). I have zero employees so no one ever calls out sick, calls with an interpersonal issue, or calls to say they forgot they have to drive their grandmother to the airport and can't come to work. No one ever requests a weekend off for their cousin's birthday, or a full week off when their nephew graduated high school, or two weeks off because their boyfriend's stepfather's tractor dealership in Indiana had an electrical fire in the showroom. (You just can't make this stuff up.)

Being a self-employed writer also means that only I decide if I am successful or not in my professional endeavors. No outsourced inspector with a clipboard ever shows up at my door unannounced to look through my business papers and check me off for all of the commas I missed. And no panicked shift supervisor ever calls me when I am halfway to Orlando with my mother to go Christmas shopping to say that the health inspector is in my store and that I have to come in right away. Never having to deal with hourly employees, ineffective change for it's own sake, or a *you missed a spot* corporate culture is worth more to my sanity and health than all of the money in the world. But there is a great deal of work that I do.

I spend twenty minutes writing out my GVA page each morning (which stands for Gratitude, Vision and

Action) and is basically my plan for my Top 4 Actions that day, and Top 4 Actions that week. Then I work for at least one hour each on at least two books that I am writing at any given time, sometimes three. I engage in internet marketing and promotion for my existing published books and update the espressoforyourgoals.com blog. Then I spend an hour or so promoting on social media and checking email. Each week I write a live music calendar for a newspaper and every other week I write a column for a newspaper. I am constantly reading books on publishing, marketing and the business of writing as well as periodically going through classic books on grammar, usage and punctuation. I also read fiction for fun. I currently have a twenty-three step marketing plan to implement for my next book and I will be doing tasks from that list while I collaborate with two freelancers who are helping me with cover and typesetting designs. I usually go to sleep around eleven p.m.

So true, I never have to "go to work". But the reality is that all I do is work. I honestly work a solid twelve hours per day, seven days a week. But if someone invites me to go to lunch or a party or a club to hear a band, I go. I exercise by walking, riding my bike or swimming everyday, and I go out in my boat whenever I feel like it. Sometimes I work in this cool coffeehouse, but I get more productive work done at home so that is my normal M.O.

The point of this is to illustrate the fact that on any given day I spend the majority of my time taking Clear Actions in the directions of my goals and visions. It just so happens that my goals and visions involve writing and publishing books and all that entails. Since I love writing this is my ideal career. The reason I work so much is because I love doing it.

I know from experience the continual challenges of working for a large company because that was my career for years. After graduating from FSU I worked for a few small companies, then for Nextel, Sprint, then Starbucks. For the last seven years of my corporate life I managed about twenty people at any given time and I wouldn't trade my experiences with those corporations for anything. But when I decided to become a self-employed writer I carefully chose my goals and affirmations based on what I did want.

Initially I was writing in my spare time while working as a manager for Starbucks full-time. My initial Main Mission that I wrote and read everyday was this:

I am financially, professionally and logistically independent and free. I earn an abundant living being who I am and doing work I love. I decide if I am successful or not in my professional endeavors. I work from wherever I choose to each day.

You see, it was partly the large corporate hierarchy that decided if I was successful or not in the large companies, and I was also not only tied to a physical location, but even when I was off I could never go far in case some emergency demanded my presence. Even on vacation, I lived with the apprehension that my phone could ring at any second to bear some stressful notion. At the same time, it was mainly the steady paycheck that kept me there (even though much of my time working was really fun). But understanding the Law of Attraction allowed me to craft my Main Mission with words describing exactly what I did want, instead of phrases about those things keeping me from it. Be sure to refrain from including the words *no, not, never* and *don't* in your ideal Destination description as you write it. For example, *"I work from wherever I choose to each day"* is a better ideal desired result than, *"I never have to be stuck in a cubicle."*

I also created my Top 4 Goals in the same way, one of them being this:

I am absolutely a published, professional self-employed writer. I write for a living and I work for myself.

I said that so many times over the course of nine months that I actually joked with my mother once by telling her that I couldn't even start to say "I am hungry," without accidentally filling in the word *hungry* with "...a published, professional, self-employed writer." That kind of passionate pursuit is the most effective way to make the Law of Attraction work for you.

Now, for me, my Main Mission and that Top 4 Goal are completely true. Every goal and person is different but it took me about nine months to go from pure idea to absolute reality. I continued to see the good in my corporate job as I built my writing and publishing business. In those days of doing both I loved the times I spent doing writing jobs and I loved my job at Starbucks because it not only allowed me to write a little, it motivated me to work my way into a position where I could write every day.

You can accomplish your goals and dreams too. Believe it. If you are just beginning, or if you are in it deep and wondering when you will finally and fully get there, have faith and remember this. When you first begin to apply the Law of Attraction, manifestation will take so long you will wonder if it is working. Once the majority of your thoughts are aligned with your intention and you believe it's possible, manifestations will happen so fast you will still wonder if it's working. (Because you will wonder if it was just a coincidence.)

So the question is not: "how long will it take a desire to manifest?" The question is: "how long will it take you to give the majority of your thoughts to the goal as achieved, and change your belief to match it?" Simply replace thoughts of doubt or lack with thoughts of belief and abundance one thought at a time. Celebrate the momentum (those moments of success) along the way. A day will come when you feel so good that you will know to a certainty that you will never go back to fretting over imaginary problems or even over real circumstances. You will know that you will never go back to your old ways of worry. That is a good day. It is the day you realize that you can indeed accomplish anything.

All of us have various degrees of connection between our passions and our work. Some of us find ourselves at the widest division (like a tax accountant who loves to play electric guitar). But even a graphic designer who loves art, and basically does art for a living, must manage through much work that is not actual art. Regardless of the exact job you maintain if your goals involve your creativity, all you have to do is give your passion some quality time. At the same time, it is always healthful to excel at your current job and doing so is a great place to apply the Law of Attraction. An automobile salesperson who likes his or her job might truly love it if they were consistently the number one salesman at their dealership. Whatever your highest goals and plans are, give their full and perfect completion more attention than you give their potential failure. Opportunities for worthy goals and skillful management of the Law of Attraction abound in every job or career. The actions that will get you to your goals fall into two main categories: Clear Actions, and Intuitive Actions.

Clear Actions, with regard to applying the Law of Attraction, are those obvious tasks that you identify on a day-to-day basis. Often they will be part of your "to do" list in the morning. These are your Top 4 Actions if you have created and use the Espresso For Your Goals system. They are those tasks or action steps that you believe will take you closer to your accomplished goals.

For example, if it is your goal to pass a Final Exam with a grade of eighty-five percent or higher, one of your Clear Actions might be to read each chapter and take your own practice test twice over the next two weeks. If your goal is to save $6,000 for a new car down payment, then your Clear Action might be to transfer $200 each pay period into your savings account.

One thing to keep in mind is this. If your goal is so large or seemingly out of reach, that your Clear Actions seem futile you might do well to scale your goal back to a reasonable stage. That is not to say you should not stretch with your goals (you should). But they have to be believable for you. Even believable goals can feel out of reach at the beginning. Therefore (when considering Clear Actions) ask yourself this: "*What would I do right now, if I knew it was impossible to fail?*" If you come up with a quick, clear answer keep following that train of thought. Allow yourself to argue against doing it a few times then keep coming back to the question. "*Yes, but if it were impossible to fail, what step would I take right now?*" If you had already worked out every resource, what one thing, out of all of the things that you would do, could you actually afford to do right now? Press on and at some point you will have to take an action.

This illustrates something profound. When you take those first steps in faith, the Universe will respond with astounding surprises. Let's say that the most money you have ever saved is $2000 cash. If, for instance, it is now your goal to save $50,000 cash over the next two years, then clearly define that goal, and make it your Clear Action to save whatever amount you can toward it, even if it's only twenty bucks a week. When you save that money by making the deposit, say to yourself, "*Here is some more money toward my fifty grand of savings.*" Then be open and expect that you will find a way to save that large amount. Little acts of faith like that pay huge dividends. Never step out on faith so far that you step into debt or take on risk beyond your wellbeing. But do what you can and would do if your goal were inevitable. The right amount of those types of actions can be rewarding beyond your wildest imagination.

The second type of action with regard to applying the Law of Attraction is an Intuitive Action. Intuitive Actions are those little nudges of impulse that come to you as you make your way through your day and week. They may not always lead you to trip over a pot of gold in the street, but quite often they can be rewarding in ways from the smallest reassurance to the most incredible, helpful *coincidence.*

Intuitive Actions are your first evidence that the game is on. They are moments when the Universe takes the opportunity to play back. I have heard it said that the old Norse Gods only died when the people forgot them. The Law of Attraction might very well feel the same way. So many people never acknowledge it working in their lives. So when someone does, the Universe delights in the attention and can not wait to play the game with you. Keep in mind, though, that size and time are nothing to the Universe. What we consider a long time is not even registered by something as eternal as the cosmos and all of it's gleaming facets. At the same time, the speed of accomplishment that the Universe is capable of is beyond instant.

There is no real way to force an Intuitive Action. Simply cultivate awareness and notice them as they arise. What you can do, however, is act on them. Acting on your intuitive notions is what fuels their effectiveness and frequency. Remember that you may not always understand or see the connections playing out to your benefit. Many times, those things and events that end up helping you are only realized long after they have played their part.

There are two ways to take advantage of these Intuitive Action opportunities and they are, in a way, opposites.

The first way is to ask your self this one question. If an intuition to take a certain action suddenly arises in your mind ask your self, *"If I did this, and everything worked out perfectly, would it take me closer to my goal?"* If the answer is yes, then you must take action. Now I am not talking about every crackpot idea that pops into your head because of some random accidental association. You have to learn how to cultivate this skill. But if you are spending a decent amount of time visualizing and affirming your goals, and taking the *clear, obvious actions* toward them each day, then you will recognize those pure, undisputed fresh ideas that spring forth into your consciousness at unexpected times.

An example of this would be from a story that I heard J.K. Rowling tell about the moment she had the idea to write the first Harry Potter book. She had been clear about her intention to write a novel. She had been searching for a subject and a fresh idea. She had written a few other stories along the way. Then one day she was riding a train somewhere in her home country of England and this thought spoke clearly in her mind: *Young boy, doesn't know he's a wizard. Goes to wizarding school.*

In hindsight we all realize and agree, *that* was a powerful Intuitive Action presenting itself. Remember, however, after that she had to write the book, and submit it to a staggering amount of agents and publishers who rejected it. She had to persist to heroic levels of belief in herself and her story before getting it published. But what would she be doing now if she had shrugged it off?

Frank Kern, one of the most successful and innovative internet marketers in history, has said that sometimes we have to suspend our own disbelief and take action anyway. What I would guess he is referring to are those moments that come to us that suggest or hint toward greater things, but refuse to outline every inch of proof.

This brings us to the second way to take advantage of intuitive nudges from the Universe. If the first way is to ask yourself if taking the action would take you closer to your goal if everything worked out, the second way is a bit more vague. You see, the second way offers no clear guess as to how the action might be important.

These Intuitive Actions are impulses that seem completely unrelated to anything you are doing or need to be doing. They seem random. As such, there are thousands of examples and none of them might ever apply. You just have to be the judge. Choose to follow your own and don't be disappointed if they seemingly lead nowhere. Remember, the workings of the Universe and it's unfailing Law of Attraction are not always cookie-cutter simple. These Intuitive Actions could be anything.

Here is an example from my own life. Take it for what it is but my hope is that this example will give you a general idea of what to look out for.

One Saturday afternoon I was headed to a have lunch at a place about forty minutes away. I chose this particular café because I like to drive, I needed to get out of my house after working in my office all week, I knew they had wi-fi, and I needed to do some internet research in hopes of finding a band to go hear live. The situation was unique because I needed to find a band for my live music column, which was due on Wednesday. Normally I would have already seen a band and been writing the article by that time, but the band I had planned to see the night before had been stuck in a Chicago airport due to snow and because of that I was stuck as well. I only had the weekend left and the pressure was on.

It was a sunny Saturday and I noticed the downtown area was filled with people walking about on the sidewalks and along the outdoor cafes in unusually high numbers. I drove around twice and found all of my normal secret parking spots filled. I decided to take one more spin back up a more heavily traveled street just for kicks. If that proved a parking bust, I would just go to the big bookstore out west (which also had a café and internet) and work from there. As I rounded the corner I saw that an arts and crafts show was in full swing. *More cars to fill spaces* I thought. Then I saw a car leaving and, even though this spot was on the opposite end of town as my coffee shop destination, something told me to take the opportunity to park. I really wasn't interested in going to the art show, but I pulled in anyway.

Since I was there I decided to stroll through the various booths. I had made a full circle and was walking back to my car, reserved to the fact that I would just head out to the big bookstore for the day. As I passed the last booth I heard a girl say, "Hey is that Les?"

I looked back to see a friend of mine buying what my brother would call "hippy soap" from a booth selling that sort of thing. I spun around and stopped to talk to her. What you have to understand is that both of us live nearly an hour from the town where the art show was and neither of us had planned to be there. When I asked this friend I had ran into what she was doing up that way she said she had visited and stayed with an old college roommate the night before and had only caught the show tents out of the corner of her eye on her drive back home.

She then asked me the same question and I explained that I was desperate to find a band playing live somewhere that weekend. I told her about my previous plan, to hear the band stuck in Chicago, and that my article's deadline was fast approaching. I explained that I had driven up to get out of the house and do some online research for bands at a certain café while having lunch, but this was the only parking I had found.

At that point my friend became quite excited and started going on and on about this amazing band she had heard twice before in Orlando. She said they were great and she was going to hear them play that very night. In fact they were playing at a venue in our home town and she insisted that I go hear them.

Now as I said, take that story for what it is. Many would see coincidence, but I see pure Law of Attraction at work through Intuitive Action. I needed a band at the last minute. I believed I would find a good band because somehow I always do (but often in the craziest ways). I set out that day with a clear intention: to find a band playing live within the next two days. My Clear Action was to go search online for bands and places they might be playing locally. Unable to find a parking place near my destination, I ended up following an Intuitive Action to park at an arts and crafts show far away just to finally park at all. I walked through the art show simply because I was there and ran smack into a friend of mine (also an hour away from home and stopping there on a whim). That friend had exactly what I needed in way of inside information on a really good band playing that night in the perfect place. I went to hear the band that night and the article came out great. I even finished it two days early. Amazing.

chapter

Being A Deliberate Creator

A Deliberate Creator is someone who recognizes the Law of Attraction at work in the natural world of their thoughts and results, and proactively applies this law to their life. A Deliberate Creator not only believes that thoughts become things, but acts accordingly. Think about that. Once you are convinced that your thoughts become what you experience, how quickly will you begin to consciously mange what you think about? How quickly will you stop complaining about what you hate and start being grateful for what you like, so that you get more of that? The answer is instantly.

Once we fully believe and understand that our most frequent and emotional thoughts become things, we stop our rants and begin to give that energy to focusing on what we want instead. When what we want is some goal or achievement, focusing more thoughts on it's accomplishment is the way to actually ensure that it gets done. The only reason any of us ever fail to do so in the first place is because (in this GPS and smartphone age) we get so hung up on having to know every step along the way, that we become afraid to begin.

When I used to work for Starbucks people would call the store I managed everyday to ask which coffees we were brewing. Really people? Live a little. It's Starbucks! It's *all* delicious. Take a chance and if you like coffee at all, drive on down here. You won't be disappointed. Deliberate Creators learn to cultivate a confident expectation based on their experience that time and time again, they get what they expect. (Pessimists cultivate this same degree of self-fulfilling prophecy, but to what end?)

So far we have covered the four stages of Deliberate Creation: Destination, Visualization, Affirmations, and Actions. In this chapter I'll give you an example project that you can adapt to something simple in your own life. Treat this as an experiment. This example will illustrate the four stages of Deliberate Creation working together in action. In short, this is your trial run to rock and roll with the game of applying the Law of Attraction.

The process of any Deliberate Creation project is the same. First you must know what it is that you want. The Destination stage consists of nailing down this ideal desired result. Then you must believe that you can accomplish it, and that you deserve it. Other teachers and writers have said that *belief* is the second step and I agree. However, how does one apply this second step of belief? By Visualization and Affirmation. Therefore, in this Apply The Law of Attraction system, the second step is Visualization. The third step is to drive your visualization home with your affirmations, or phrases that describe your goal as already accomplished. Together, these second and third steps combine to generate the beliefs that you need to move ahead. It's the feeling of your intention that attracts like feelings to you. When you activate the feeling of your ideal desired result in your imagination, the Universe responds with experiences that match it. It does so by matching your frequencies with the vibrational energy that makes up all material things. Remember, no one outside of your self is making a decision about what you get. It is simply an energetic Universe responding to an energetic thought and feeling. That's why you get what you think and feel the most often, rather than what you imagine for a second or two that you deserve.

Over time your habitual thoughts and feelings create enough experiences that those experiences color your attitude. Your attitude could be said to be your expectations, and therefore an aspect of your beliefs. In fact, attitude and affirmations have the power to update your beliefs to match your ideal desired result without any time spent banishing or fussing with your old limiting beliefs to the contrary.

The fourth step is to take action toward your goals. Exactly what action might seem vague, but take action anyway and get moving. It is this motion that will call into your experience the next, more obvious steps. Also, as you are considering actions, remember to take those Intuitive Actions that might seem random, but that will often lead you to unseen aid and surprise opportunities.

Let's get into our experimental example so we can begin to take the Law of Attraction on a trial run. If this is new territory to you, begin small. Choose an ideal desired result that is believable, yet that you may have struggled with in the past. A doable project, but one you think you have procrastinated on, is the perfect place to experiment with applying the process of Deliberate Creation. For example, let's say that you have been trying to make time to paint your garden shed. Your ideal desired result might be: *"The garden shed is painted 100% and looks great."*

Consider your thoughts on that project over the last month or so. For instance, have you found yourself saying, *"I need to finish painting the garden shed. I can't believe I haven't found time to do that yet,"* or something similar?

Replace those ideas with something like, *"I am so*

happy now that the garden shed is totally painted. It looks just like I had imagined it to!" Every time you say that, picture it perfectly finished in your mind for a second.

Then just go about your week. Don't try to force doing the job. Just listen to your thoughts on the subject. Have fun with it. Pretend you are a magician and your thoughts will accomplish it. Hey, you've already put it off for a month, so what's the rush now, right?

Visualize it as done for five minutes per day. For now don't try to do it right or worry about doing it wrong. Just hold in your imagination, what you think the painted shed will look like for five little minutes in a row once a day. You can do it.

Then, as your week goes on, when you hear yourself say something like, *"Man, I still need to finish painting that damn garden shed,"* (and don't worry, you will have that thought,) stop yourself and replace it with the thought of your ideal desired result: *"I am so happy now that the garden shed is totally painted."*

The first time you do this, it will feel absurd. Your old thought habits will laugh. That's fine. Just repeat your phrase and then keep going with your day. As you progress through your week, persistently replace *"I need to finish,"* or *"I can't believe I haven't yet,"* thoughts with *"I am so happy now that* [whatever it is you're trying to do] *is so perfectly completed."* It could very well be painting the garden shed, but it might be fixing your riding lawnmower, beginning a school project that isn't due for a month, or making an actual scrapbook out of all those pictures scattered around on your computer, phone, and in boxes in your closet. For this example we will stick to the garden shed, but insert your own project's details as we go.

So when you have those thoughts of what you should have done already, replace them with your ideal desired result phrase. Cultivate the attitude that you will succeed. Then also throw a few of your ideal desired result phrases in there even when you are having no doubts at all. Very quickly this thought will feel at home in your mind and you might not even remember procrastinating about it (or feeling like you were). Even though you haven't taken any physical action to do the job yet, the feeling of it being done is creeping into your thought pattern. This is a joyful moment. Press on.

When you start to feel more comfortable saying your version of *"I am so happy now that the garden shed is totally painted,"* than worrying about needing to do it, get ready. Be on the look out because "How" is about to join the party. It may be an extra day to yourself that you had not planned on. Perhaps it's a kid's canceled soccer game, or a change in your spouse's plan that leaves you with an entire sunny day of free time. Or you might find the Home Depot gift card that your annoying mother in-law gave you on your birthday, but you had forgotten that you had.

When this situation presents itself, you will say, *"I wonder if this is a coincidence?"*

That thought is the fluorescent red flag! When you have it ask yourself this one question: If I acted on this opportunity now, and used it to take this step, would it take me any closer to my goal being fulfilled? If the answer is yes, then you have to take action. Your action will reinforce your own belief in the Deliberate Creation process. Do it.

Once you begin it, you will be amazed at how quickly it all works out. Just push on and finish the job. Part of you will say, *"Well of course it's done now. I did all that stuff to actually do the task."*

Yes this will be true, but compare your result to the weeks or months of putting it off. A day or two later when it's all said and done, find a quiet moment to your self. Breathe deep a few times and clear your mind. When you feel relaxed and calm I want you to do something for me. (And ultimately for you of course.) In that calm, quiet, relaxed state, when you have finally completed that thing that you had not for so long, I want you to say out loud your version of our phrase:

> **"I am so happy now that the garden shed is totally painted. It looks just like I had imagined it to!"**

Please, truly and actually do this. The rush of energy you will feel in that moment will blow your mind. From that moment on your life will never be the same. You will know too much and your thoughts of doubt will never hold the same power. You will know that you can accomplish anything. So, yes, you may have to work. You may have to strive. You may have to learn new skills and apply yourself. But you would have to do that anyway and all that effort might have been sabotaged by thoughts like, *"I can't believe,"* *"What if I fail?"* or *"I still need to."* Not anymore. You are now prepared to become a champion Deliberate Creator. You are unstoppable.

* * *

In the next chapter we will embark into the fascinating territory of equal vibrations and learn how to steer a course using the law of resonance. I have found that the more I look into the Law of Attraction, the more it reveals. The further I explore, the deeper it goes. I have been studying this process for quite some time and it continually amazes and delights in unexpected ways.

Chapter 7

The Law Of Resonance

As Deliberate Creators we know that thoughts become things. There are many ways to describe the process of putting Deliberate Creation into practice. In this book we have begun the Deliberate Creation journey by recognizing and following four stages: Destination (clearly define it), Visualization (picture and feel it), Affirmation (believe it), and Actions (move toward it). So in the purest analysis, that's all you have to do.

Define what you want, visualize it as completed until you feel good about it, affirm it until you believe it, take the Clear Actions toward it that are obvious, then follow the Intuitive Actions that feel right in the moment.

Once you get the hang of it following the four stages of Deliberate Creation will consistently put you in a place of receiving. This chapter will give you some more advanced receiving tools. When you first set out to apply the Law of Attraction you will spend some time realizing the thoughts you have consistently driven in the past, and all the ways those old thought patterns have created the reality that you find your self in now. It's natural to recognize these connections, because you are looking for some proof in those early days of joining the Law of Attraction Tribe, as I am so fond of calling it.

As you reflect on experiences you have had in the past, you may have a few that really stand out. Cherish those things that worked out well. If you can recall a time when you got something almost exactly the way you wanted it, revel in the memory every now and then. Those feelings will bring more similar feeling times into your life.

You may also have a few situations that confound your most sincere reasoning. All logic and circumstance might point to your accomplishment of something, yet, for whatever reason, you just can't ever seem to get it done. In my experience those situations are caused by one of two things nearly ninety percent of the time. The other ten percent accounts for the fact that the experience of life is so complex that we can never truly understand the reasons behind every circumstance. However, in cases when all logical reason would indicate your success in a certain area, yet you just never seem to achieve it, my observation has been that it has two possible main causes. First, these times can be the result of the fact that sometimes the Universe just knows better. I think we have all heard the notion that sometimes God's greatest gifts are unanswered prayers. (I think that might even be a line in a country song.) But often those types of catch phrases persist because of a certain amount of truth. I, for one, have definitely had the experience of wanting something that I thought I deserved, like a specific job, only to discover a less qualified candidate got it. In the moment it seemed like an injustice, but later I realized the event to be in my best interest when I was able to move on to something better. Maybe it's that one girl or guy you really wanted, but that turned out to be a drag and a burden for the person they ended up with (and whom you were initially jealous of). Or maybe it is a creative goal, like writing a book or starting a business that just feels long overdue. This first reason (of an unanswered prayer being a gift) just might be the cause.

Secondly (and this reason is one that is under your control) is the fact that you may have been giving more of your thought to your goal's absence by being so astounded that you haven't achieved it yet. That can be a powerful emotion and when emotions are involved in thoughts, the Law of Attraction responds with even more accuracy and speed. Remember that the Law of Attraction is simply a natural force. It is indifferent to what you do or don't accomplish. The Law of Attraction is not a fancy name for an invisible human personality. It does not judge. It's just the way that an interconnected field of constituent energy aligns the complimentary energies or vibrations within itself. It is just the way that energy works. Think of it like this. If a bucket of water is poured onto someone, that person will get wet. It doesn't matter if it is a good person or a bad person. Water makes you wet without distinction. It's just the way water works. In the same way, the Law of Attraction gives you what you give the majority of your thought, emotion and belief to. It does not matter if you are focusing on your goal accomplished, or on the fact that *there is no way that I have not gotten this done yet.* It is the vibration of your thought or belief that the Law of Attraction responds to. The thought and feeling of *I can't believe this goal is still not accomplished* is the same vibration as *this goal is not accomplished.* The more attention you give that vibration, the more evidence of it you get in your experience.

The way you manage your way around those times is by remembering to focus on what you *do* want at least more often than on the evidence of its absence.

At this point you have done the *heavy lifting* as a dear friend of mine, and fellow high achiever, says. Remind yourself that once you have the four stages of Deliberate Creation up and running, your only job is to *equate* your feelings to the same feelings as your intention fulfilled. Resist the temptation to try to orchestrate your entire manifestation. Don't *micromanage* the Law of Attraction. Yes, there are times for lists and Clear Actions. But resonance functions through aligned frequencies. In keeping with the heavy lifting analogy, think of it like this. Once you have moved a piano into its ideal spot, you don't have to move it around again every day to get it there. You just walk into your music room (remember, think big people) and there it is just where you wanted it. Your big goals are the same way. Spend the time and effort putting them where you want them, or in other words, defining them clearly as done. Then know they are right and give your energy to feeling them as done. Feeling them as done is making use of the law of resonance.

The law of resonance seems to be making a big splash in our LOA Tribe lately and I honestly think it's because, at some point, Law of Attraction coaches and writers run out of things to talk about. That's why it is just a chapter in this book and not an entire book unto itself. Essentially the law of resonance and the Law of Attraction say the same thing. The argument is that the law of resonance is *how* the Law of Attraction works, but then search for a definition of the law of resonance and it basically says that energies of the same tone attract each other and vibrate together at the same frequency. That sounds quite similar to *like attracts like* to me, and it is exactly that. However, there are some aspects to the law of resonance that reinforce the way the Law of Attraction functions and they are valuable and bear inclusion in this, our Apply The Law of Attraction manual.

Resonance happens when a specific vibration stimulates an equally tuned latent subject. Just like two walkie-talkies must be on the same channel for a message transmitted from one to be received by the other. So, too, must the thoughts and feelings that you focus your desires on match the circumstances, people and events that find their way into your life. How do you know the vibration of having your goal fulfilled if you have never achieved it yet? The answer is that the Law of Attraction (and its technical cousin the law of resonance) is more forgiving than a radio transmitter. Radio equipment is designed to divide radio spectrum discretely so we get no interference. But the law of resonance functions, in the realm of human experience, on a wider scale. In fact, you can think of the law of resonance as having only two really wide channels with regard to tuning into feelings. One channel feels good. The other channel feels bad.

That's as specific as you need to get. Yes there are more subtle energies at work, but there is no need to stress over defining and recognizing them all. That would be the micromanaging tendency we talked about resisting.

The best way to understand what the law of resonance looks like at work is to go through a few real world examples. If you have ever seen a beautiful, gleaming natural crystal then you are seeing a physical creation of the law of resonance. Those shining caves of hollow rock lined with purple amethyst crystals, or dazzling clusters of ice-clear quartz always amaze me. To me they are more beautiful than the finest jewelry made by man. And to think, they formed of themselves, without any person arranging, carving or dying them.

The way that such crystals form is through a process where the conditions of the air and minerals are allowed (for centuries in some cases) to exist undisturbed. In these tranquil environments, if all of the necessary components are in attendance, a single molecule will attach to the wall of a stone. In the cave-dark stillness, if another molecule of the exact same type happens by it will join the first. Once two are together it is natural for a third to attach with them. Leave that process alone for a few hundred years and an elaborate crystal will materialize. The astounding thing is that the overall shape of the crystal's faceted points will always be an exact mirror of the shape of the repetitive molecules that form it. To view a natural crystal is to view the Law of Attraction functioning through the law of resonance.

Another more human example is the behavior of children. Have you ever heard a teacher or parent say that one kid is a bad influence on another? If you have, or are around, kids for any amount of time, then you have seen the law of resonance in action. One of the most fascinating things I have ever witnessed in this regard is the moment when a toddler first encounters another child of his or her same age. Often children of three or four years old have not had long interactions with other children their same size and age. If you have ever witnessed two young children encounter one another for the first time then you have witnessed life's magic. And I am not referring to two children who have just never met before. I'm talking about that moment when two young ones who have never *seen* another person their same size and age all of a sudden see each other. If the two are somewhere that interaction is easy and safe, like at the beach or in a park or something, watch how fast they gravitate toward each other. You won't be able to keep them apart. Their actions are spontaneous and they just run up to each other and begin to interact.

To make use of this energy all you have to do is remember that the law of resonance only has two frequencies worth worrying about: good and bad. As you consider your intentions move into the world of action and be mindful of how your ideas and observations make you feel. If you are feeling good, then keep going. Let your good feelings guide you toward more good feelings as you focus on your ideal desired results. Good feelings generate (and are generated by) thoughts of excitement, confidence, readiness, abundance and happiness. If, when you focus on your goal, you naturally have those types of thoughts and feelings, then you are on the right track.

If, on the other hand, you find your highest goals cause thoughts and feelings of stress, disappointment, lack or sadness then refocus toward their completion and not their absence. Often these negative vibrations just make an appearance for a second. Fine. Just let them come and go like the chattering of crows on the wire. It is just noise. Yes it has a place, but its place is not in the majority of your time and attention. The reason for bad feelings is to alert you to focus on good feelings instead. Negative feelings and thoughts point toward things you do not want. Allow them to remind you to focus, instead, on what you actually do want. Simply search for the feeling of happiness that your goal accomplished will give you. Release the habit of focusing on what a drag it is that your goal is still a hope or dream. The Law of Attraction always delivers. It always works. It simply delivers to you, what you *resonate* with the most often and the most passionately.

Recognize the dazzling moments of the law of resonance in the world. Use it as fuel to manage and actualize your highest dreams and goals by applying the Law of Attraction toward more of what you want than more of what you don't.

One of the easiest and most effective ways to harness the power of the law of resonance (and by definition the Law of Attraction) is the old *act as if* routine. It can also be really fun. Pick one of your highest goals or intentions and choose something you can do in order to *act as if* you have already accomplished it. Don't go so far as to put yourself in debt over it, but if your true goal is to double your income, then splurge when you can afford it even in the most subtle way. If you like good beer to go with your sushi, then buy the more expensive Japanese import beer at the sushi place. It's only one dollar more than the cheapest beer on the menu. One dollar. You loose that much running for the bus. But use that tiny indulgence as a moment to savor the feelings of abundance. Something I like to do is always donate to whatever charity my local grocery store is collecting for when I shop. When I come up to pay and the cashier asks if I would like to donate to the XYZ fund to help kids or what have you, I always say yes and give them a buck. If I were focused on lack and therefore clinging to every penny I would say no. Doing so would send the *I lack money* signal to the Universe and I would get more experiences to prove it. But since my goal is abundance I act as if I have more money than I need in that instant so, *sure, I'll donate today.* Remember, I don't act like I have more money than I need and go finance a Lamborghini (yet). But I will donate a dollar for little kids when I buy groceries. I have done that at my most broke moment and with pleasure because I know that what you give is what you get.

When you *act as if* it sends a signal to the Universe, which always responds in kind. This shows the difference in the power of action as it relates to resonance and, therefore, alignment. Thinking you are rich, saying you are rich and visualizing you are rich all send vibrations to fuel the Law of Attraction. But being too cheap to donate a dollar to starving kids, or using a calculator to subtract sales tax from a dinner bill so you are relieved from the responsibility of tipping on that extra seven percent sends a much more powerful message. Goal set, visualize and affirm? Yes. But also *act* as if you are there already in the little ways you can each day.

Another thing I used to do to act as if I was a completely self-employed writer (well before I was) was this. On my days off from my corporate job I would pack up my notebooks and laptop and drive up the coast to Melbourne, Florida, which is just about forty minutes away. I would spend the day writing at this cool little café in the old downtown area just because part of my Main Mission back then was to be able to work from wherever I chose to each day. I would do my best to forget my day job and, for that afternoon, be a self-employed author. If someone asked me what I was up to (coffee shop people love to talk to strangers sometimes) I would say that I was a writer. The fact was that I was a writer, even a paid one to a degree. I would just leave out the part about me working forty-five hours a week at my other job.

Now when I feel like getting out of the house I will often go to that same café to work. I always have to laugh to myself. The fine people who work there have never known my struggles and long hours of doing both a corporate job and striving to reach my self-employment goals. They only know me as the guy who is a writer. That's whom they knew me as when it was only a dream, and that's whom they know me as now that it is a pure reality. For that very reason I love that place. Maybe if they ask me what I'm up to now I will say that I'm working on topping the New York Times Bestseller List. The barista there would probably say, "Oh cool. Well enjoy your espresso."

Acting as if is a powerful way to resonate at the same

vibration as your intended ideal desired result. Also remember that once you realize that your goal seems overdue, it could likely be for one of two main reasons. Sometimes it is your unanswered prayer and sometimes it is because you have passionately given too much energy to the illogical fact that you have not accomplished something yet. Be cautious of continually resonating at the same frequency as your goal unfulfilled. Recognize these moments as times when invisible forces are still assembling and continue to give your energy toward feeling the same state as your goal achieved.

Increase your enthusiasm about the steps toward your goal that you have accomplished so far, to such a degree that the steps you have not achieved yet become irrelevant. Not irrelevant to accomplish, but irrelevant with regard to how their absence makes you feel. You are simply on the journey. *Act as if* and *believe* in your goals so that you can continue until you *receive* your goals.

chapter 8

Lulls, Doubts And Resistance

In the golden age of exploration one of the most feared events was a big storm at sea. In tropical waters that were thousands of miles and months from civilization, hurricanes, tropical depressions and even good old-fashioned thunderstorms could spell at the very least delays, damaged cargo or broken gear and at worst a shipwreck. Yet even for the fearsome wrath of those heavy storms, another event caused just as much dread: the doldrums.

Sailing ships crossing the Atlantic often encountered areas of atmospheric conditions where wind literally ceased for days or even weeks at a time. With no headway, and often no rain to go with it, supplies and patience would dwindle as dissatisfaction and tempers would rise.

Similar experiences of lull in forward momentum are often encountered as we journey along the trade routes of Deliberate Creation, although perhaps not to such a dramatic consequence.

As proactive applicants of the Law of Attraction, we must be exceedingly cautious in such times of lull. For, our thoughts are the very winds that propel us (or the very confirmation of the stillness that strands us). If we begin to give more of our attention to this lack of progress, then guess what we will get more of?

In such times, when it seems that nothing is happening, remember that the little miracles of the Universe that align to help your cause are nearly always unseen as they occur. Lulls are the times when the Universe is arranging things. Follow your Clear and Intuitive Actions and just keep going. You are still moving toward your goal through the passage of time. Just because things seem slow or overdue does not mean there is a problem. It is just that those things that are being shifted around to help you take time and we don't always see them.

We only recognize many coincidences that took place in our favor from a position of hindsight. This is the time when you must have faith in the process. You must still allow your goal to reach you, even when you can't see it coming. The only thing that will push it away is doubt. Can you doubt? Yes and as humans we always will. It isn't one or two doubts that do us in. However, giving more attention and energy to doubts than to success most certainly will. In other words, allowing is nothing more than the absence of fear, or doubt.

You can begin allowing by focusing on thoughts that displace the doubts in your mind. Belief is the absence of doubt. Faith is the absence of doubt. Certainty is the absence of doubt. Confidence is the absence of doubt. Consider your thought and how it makes you feel. In general, if your thoughts make you feel good about your goal, you are on the right track. If your goal conjures feelings of disappointment and regret, reboot and go for something better.

Lulls and doubts do not have to go together because you can use lulls as times to reflect and prepare for the good to come. Just remember that lulls and doubts are old friends. It is easy for them to get together again. You can even let them, but for just long enough to keep your feet on the ground. If it's your intention to accomplish your goal, then refocus on that, and let doubt fade away to the margins where it belongs.

At this stage we will get into a subject that is actually a concentrated version of doubt: resistance. Resistance is active purposeful doubt. Sometimes it is our own, but often it is presented to us through the attitudes and beliefs of others. Typically it is someone we know and trust to some degree, or the resistance would either be unknown or irrelevant.

Resistance is one way that other people's thoughts or opinions can influence our own. It is so important, therefore, to surround ourselves with positive people who believe in us and who will be champions for our goals. If there are none of those people around then you go it alone for a while.

But just relax and be yourself. This is not something you have to constantly manage. The elegant Law of Attraction will make sure that you gravitate toward those who equate to your vibrational offering. We always have to make choices about where and with whom we spend time. But you will also find that when you are focused on your goals, and living the valid, joyful life you deserve, those who would discourage you become basically absent. Your paths will simply fail to cross as often and it is because you are on opposite wavelengths. At the same time, if you have an inclination to reach out to an old friend who may have faded from your circle of experience for a time, do so. Very often you may find that their perspective has changed and you are, once again, compatible and can move ahead together. Remember, all of us have the capacity to grow, change, and improve our selves and our lives. (Even those who, on the surface, would seem to scoff at your ability to do so.)

But what if the person offering resistance or criticism is your significant other, your parent, or your roommate and you can't actually avoid them? In that instance you must carefully choose what to share with them about your Deliberate Creation projects. Yes we must be honest with the people in our lives, but we must also be respectful of our own personal growth and health. If the person you are involved with does not respect your goals and dreams, then *you* must. Keep your highest intentions safe from undue criticism. Also you can always orient your own thoughts and feelings toward the best parts of the person. Don't automatically expect them to be against your plans or dreams. Carefully choose what you share about your goals and focus your thoughts on the positive attributes of your resistant-prone acquaintance. We hear this all the time in Law of Attraction discussions and even in general self-help and motivational thinking. It is a recurring theme because of the fact that other people's thoughts can influence our own point of attraction, even though it is always only our thoughts, not theirs, that have impact. Here is just one hypothetical example of how the thoughts of others can affect our point of attraction, or the vibration we are offering.

Let's say that someone close to you doesn't believe in your goal, vision or something that you are setting out to do. Basically they don't believe you can do it. Then you find out about their statement or belief either first-hand, or from someone else (which would probably be a very common avenue for that type of information to travel).

So there you are. You have a goal and a vision that you are trying to manifest. You are working with the Law of Attraction to believe in yourself and believe in the outcome. Then you hear that someone you know, value, trust and/or love doesn't think that you can do it. The first thing you are likely to say is, "*Well I really don't care what they think.*"

Then an hour later you begin to imagine yourself having a conversation with that person, arguing your side of it, trying to explain your goal better—*stop right there!*

When that happens, that is how you know they are influencing you. Their idea and negative attitude is influencing your point of attraction when you mentally entertain a discussion with them about failing. In that situation immediately stop, delete, reformat the hard drive, go through your affirmations a few times then call it a day.

The point is this: we imagine that the opinions of others don't affect us, however, if the other person is someone we are close to then their opinions can. You just have to be cautious when this happens. One way you know that this is happening is when you start to have those imaginary arguments with this person after the fact.

Remember (and thank the Universe for it) that their attitude and belief has absolutely no bearing on your accomplishment unless you let it by giving their negative thoughts *more* attention than you give to your own confident expectations.

Think of resistance like this:

What do you think has more influence on what you do or do not accomplish, your thoughts, or the thoughts and opinions of someone who thinks you can't do something?

One way to realize the truth that *the thoughts of others have no bearing on your achievement* is to take the analogy to an extreme level. Imagine someone that you admire as powerfully successful in his or her field, then imagine your naysaying friend speaking some resistant opinion directly to that person. (This can actually be really fun.) Imagine, for instance, that Robert Dinero just agreed to play the part in a new movie, and picture your doubtful friend meeting him and saying, "I don't think you will ever be good enough to play that part convincingly." What would Dinero say? Or imagine your friend going up to Anthony Robbins or Oprah and saying, "I heard about what you've decided to do, and I honestly don't think you can accomplish something like that." Ha! That's ridiculous, right? Well it's just as ridiculous that anyone's opinion could ever truly determine what you can or cannot accomplish.

In fact sometimes a little resistance can be a powerful motivator. My mother might tell you that the most sure-fire way to get me to accomplish something difficult, when I was a kid, would have been to suggest that I might not be able do it. Back then they just called that condition *hard-headed*. And my grandmother always said that I had a *wild imagination* if I told her what I wanted to do or be someday. Well as it turns out that is actually a pretty sweet combination of character for getting some serious accomplishment done. In fact I think it would make a fantastic job description for the highest achievers: *the ideal candidate for this position will be a hard-headed deliberate creator with a wild imagination.*

When someone tells you your goal is impossible take that moment and file it away. Use it to add to your confidence by telling yourself, *"I can't **wait** to remind them of that comment once this is done."* In fact, pull that into your visualization routine now and then. Vividly imagine yourself casually bringing it up in front of your resisting friend and a few other people. Just use it to your advantage and give more of your thoughts to situations

Lulls, Doubts and Resistance

that will only occur once your goal is a done deal. Little gems like that can be Law of Attraction gold nuggets.

I have heard it explained that an airplane must go *against* the wind in order to take off. Maybe as Deliberate Creators we need a little resistance also to help us gain some ground at certain times. In fact, when writing this very book it was the resistance of those who discount the Law of Attraction that I used to frame the logical arguments for its efficacy. When doing so I imagined that some of my stories or examples might someday give someone that small amount of extra confidence they needed to push on one more day toward their goal and then hit it. Remember that no matter what lulls, doubts or resistance you encounter, that every day is a day closer to your fully realized ideal desired result.

chapter

Tools Of The Trade

This chapter is simply a brief listing of some of my favorite Law of Attraction tools. These are easy, fun, yet powerful methods to get more bang from your Deliberate Creation efforts.

The Road Exercise

This is a very advanced technique for applying the Law of Attraction and as such, it should be approached and used with the utmost mindfulness and caution. It is also one of the most powerful which is why I have placed it first in this Tools Of The Trade chapter.

So much of successful Deliberate Creation involves striving to focus on your dreams more than your fears.

Indeed that is what success looks like along the way. It is what gets you there. However, sometimes we must honestly and directly confront our current situation and our past performance in order to effectively chart a course away from it.

You will recognize the need for this tool when you find yourself at a very critical stage mentally (that is critical as far as your thoughts and therefore your ultimate results are concerned). These times can arise after you have given a heroic effort toward some goal or desire, only to be drastically disappointed in the initial results. In such an instance you can use this Road Exercise to clearly and passionately define the contrast (or poor result) as well as everything you poured into it up to this point. This definition is only in the interest of being honest with your self, for the purpose of choosing the path away from what you don't want.

To implement the Road Exercise write out two paragraphs to be labeled one and two. In paragraph one describe all you have been through and invested in your effort to achieve this certain goal or intention. Clearly and powerfully describe the work you have done as well as the poor results you have experienced so far. Be honest and accurate. Describe the situation truly as it is (but not worse than it is). Label this paragraph one, then skip a line or two to write paragraph two.

In paragraph two write out in gleaming detail all of the descriptions and statistics of what your experience would be if your efforts had met or exceeded your expectations. This exercise works best for intentions and goals that take a while to play out. But those long-term projects or dreams are also the most susceptible to mid-term disappointment that you can still do something about, and therein lay both the need and potential effectiveness of this tool.

Finish paragraph two to the best of your ability to describe, once again, our old friend your ideal desired result. Label it paragraph two, then read both paragraphs. Consciously choose and declare to follow the course toward that which paragraph two describes. Write down your commitment to do so.

This is, as I mentioned, a very advanced tool. Like the sharpest of knives it must be handled with equal parts of caution and confidence. As such, it is also one of the most powerful exercises you can employ. It gives you the ability to clearly understand that whatever lack of achievement, poor performance or disagreeable situation you find yourself confronting is not where you are. It is where you were. Define it in the clearest terms but only once. Know it to be true but true like the road that brought you here and not worth backtracking up if you still wish to get to your destination.

Remember our analogy from Chapter Two about the ideal desired result being one possible direction on the same long straight road? That is the origin of this tool's name. Paragraph one is your glance back toward the direction you do not want to go further in. Then using those paragraph one perspectives, statistics and viewpoints clearly describe the road leading in the opposite direction. Passionately describe the pinnacle of accomplishment still to be realized because of all of your previous section of that road's investment. The first paragraph is the long straight road behind you. The second paragraph is the long straight road ahead of you. Consciously choose to only follow the road ahead.

From this moment forward, use these two paragraphs like you would use a navigational chart that depicts a dangerous reef to the south and that one particular harbor to the north. You have charted the reef so you can avoid it, not dwell upon it. When you have thoughts of discouragement resulting from your experience of disappointment described in paragraph one, read paragraph two and remember your conscious choice to only sail toward that.

Do not give up now. Know that this is the point where so many others have given up before you. At this stretch of your journey the dark sea floor below you is littered with the bones of ghosts who have given up in despair. The shipwrecks of their remnant dreams call for you to join their woeful armada. Tip your hat to those lost souls with the understanding that they too tried their best. But you are equipped with an urgent errand and a clear vision. You know that the wake of a ship does not propel it. You have chosen to accurately define the danger behind you, only so that you may safely and surely sail away from it. Do so by reading the paragraph of your cherished destination and choose to head in that direction with all your future thoughts.

The Smartphone Audio Recorder

Maybe the app you have is called an audio recorder, voice recorder, or voice memo gadget. Whatever it's called, it is LOA gold. Yes we have had portable recorders for generations now, but the smartphone just makes it so continually available. Just like the ubiquitous camera, the voice recorder is with us nearly all the time these days. Make use of it. One of the most powerful things you can do is use it to first record your top goals, then listen to them periodically. In addition, you can record your affirmations and play them back in the same way. I have a cord that plugs into the stereo in my car so I can listen to my recordings as I drive. This functions on the same principle of repetition that reading goals or affirmations does, but hearing them stimulates different areas of your brain. A human voice, particularly your own, can have dramatic impact on your feelings. Use this impact to your benefit.

Physical Checklists With an Action Component

Checklists are probably the oldest and most basic tool for getting anything done. A list is good because it allows you to plan out multiple tasks so that you first, remember them all, and second, do them in order if that is important.

When making lists for Deliberate Creation it is important to remember not to try to force *how* into every intention by including your preconceived notions into each goal or intention by way of a list. Lists for Deliberate Creators are reserved for top-level obvious tasks. Tasks that you know must get done in order for a dream to manifest. For instance, if your goal is to publish a novel, you know you have to write one. Your checklist might include writing one chapter per day.

The action component of your list is important. By action component I mean some mechanism that you employ to indicate accomplishment. Personally, I make a little empty box to the left of each item on my Top 4 Actions each day and each week. As I do the task or action,

I check the box off. Looking at my list I can get a quick visual understanding of how much I have accomplished on any given day. I know people who put their actions on sticky notes, then enjoy the feeling of satisfaction they get by pulling the note down and crumbling it up or shredding it. Done!

The Portable Vision Board

The Portable Vision Board tool might be self-explanatory, but allow me to describe mine, the reason for it and how I use it to my advantage.

First let me say that getting away from your vision board can actually be a good thing. There are times when too much focus on such a tool can send messages of desperation in your Law of Attraction career. If looking at your vision board feels like a chore, or gives you a feeling of disappointment, then consider it an indication of such times. Put it away for a while then return to it later when it feels right.

That being said, there are also times when you are on a visualizing roll, and you don't want to loose that momentum. Being a self-employed writer I often like to travel since I can basically work from anywhere there is electricity. An internet connection is nice, but I don't even really need that to write. I actually write freehand sometimes just to get stuff out fast or if inspiration strikes when my trusty laptop is not around, so I don't even have to always have electricity.

Right now I am planning a trip to Saint Augustine, Florida to spend a month working on a series of fiction novels (The Witch Shop Trilogy) that is set in that city. Lately I have been so thrilled to have moved some of my long-term goals from the Vision side of my board to the Success Board side. While I am away I want to keep that creative river flowing, so it is the perfect time to take along my Portable Vision Board.

My Portable Vision Board is made on the inside of a manila file folder. Folded closed it takes up the same thin space as a virtually empty file. Inside I have color copies of pictures that illustrate my Top 4 Goals and Top 4 Visions, as well as sticky notes of my Main Mission, Top 4 Goals, and Top 4 Visions in written form. I can prop the opened file up on a desk or table and use it to visualize my goals as achieved for a few minutes everyday. It is just a simple, but powerful way to keep the process of using a vision board going as you travel.

Try making your own and see if you like using it. It isn't for carrying everywhere and overdoing the process. But a bit of well-timed preparation can often pay huge dividends in momentum and consistency as you hone your Deliberate Creator skills.

The Internet

Really? Did he just say *the internet?* Well actually, yes, I did. I was brainstorming my favorite Law of Attraction tools and the good old internet is most definitely one. We live in an information age where access to ideas, thoughts and recorded works of all description is at its highest point in history. The entire Universe is made up of energy and the internet is no exception. Consider an eBook. It is written using electrical signals and data in a computer. It is advertised, sold, and delivered over the internet with the energy of electricity. It is purchased with an electronic transfer of funds and read on an electrical device. The thoughts that you consume as you read it become electrical impulses in your brain and as you write about it on social media you are connecting electronically with the entire web of computers across the planet. Search engines function the same way and all of it amounts to a giant electronic exoskeleton for the planet.

Admittedly it can have the feeling of trying to drink water from a fire hose, but there is no denying that the internet can be a powerful Law of Attraction tool. Often when I feel stalled or need some good old-fashioned Law of Attraction random input, I will dial up my trusty internet and search for something more or less related to what I am trying to accomplish. I will jump around from images to videos to articles and blogs. Sometimes it's a bust. But other times I will find my way to *exactly* the right bit of information that solves my dilemma and also adds something extra to my situation. It's really exciting to find these little jewels of help. Using the internet in this way is probably one of those things that you just have to learn how to do for yourself at a certain point, but I think you get the picture.

The more I employ this seemingly sketchy tool, the more I realize that the widespread availability of the internet and the growing enthusiasm for the Law of Attraction absolutely go hand in hand. They are two active, living ideas who's time has come and together they can take each other to incredible heights of rapid potential. The next time you feel lost or in need of something unknown for your Deliberate Creation path, jump on the internet and do a few related but random searches that are in the same ballpark as whatever it is you are working on. You may be amazed at the pristine, gleaming value that you discover. You may also waste three hours watching squirrels waterski, but that's just the chance you take on the internet these days. Good luck!

Random Reaches

The internet "tool" above might just be the electronic version of my old standby *Random Reaches*. I happen to be of an age that I still have a library of actual books in my house. Books that I cherish, books that I have nearly memorized, and books that I forgot that I had. I have never actually counted them but I bet I have at least five hundred. Those books cover quite an array of subjects both fiction and otherwise. They are the perfect medium for a Random Reach. Sometimes if I have an unsolvable question or even if I just want to see what happens I will go to one of my shelves and pull a Random Reach. Grab a book, open it and start reading. This can be astounding. Not always, but it can be. You can also do a Random Reach in a bookstore or almost anywhere, like the magazine rack in a grocery store. All you are doing is trusting the Universe in some strange way. You are saying, *okay, I give up. Hit me with your best shot*.

Random Reaches can be done in a multitude of ways. Books and other written material seem to lend themselves perfectly to the tool. But be on the lookout for help in the strangest places. Have you ever gotten that one most profound fortune cookie? This is the same idea. It is an action based on the slightest (or strongest) bit of faith and it also falls into that category of *can't hurt, might help.* Remember this is not the entire book here. It is only one suggested tool to help you begin to understand the strange ways that the Law of Attraction can often operate. I think it's more about your receiving than the medium. Try a Random Reach sometime and see what you come up with.

Fast Forward Journaling

Fast Forward Journaling is also included in Espresso For Your Goals, but it warrants a space in this chapter as well. The benefit of this goal accomplishment tool is in its multilayered nature. It can help you achieve powerful results because it works on so many levels at once. Once you understand how to do it, it almost becomes second nature. It uses the power of *acting as if your goal is achieved* to help you give thoughts and energy to your ideal desired result. The more thought and emotion you give to the feeling of your ideal desired result, the more you fuel the Law of Attraction.

Fast Forward Journaling is powerful because it is handwritten, comes from the perspective of completion, and is something that many people already do (journaling that is). The process is easy and fun. Simply write out a single page from the perspective of a day when your goal is done and living. Pretend you are in the future and this is really your journal entry for whatever is happening in your life. Allow yourself to write freely. Rejoice. Remember. Complain. Plan. Reflect. There is no right or wrong thing to say, as long as you write as if your goal or goals are already achieved and active in your experience. Try it and it just might blow you away someday when you look back on some of your entries and see how accurate they actually were.

chapter 10

Ancient Secrets Of Magic

The term magic, as we will discuss it here, is used to denote a type of practical application of natural energies to accomplish a specific act of will or volition. Unlike stage magic where rabbits are pulled from hats, ancient magic was both a religion and a science. Magicians were the wisest of men. In fact, the very word *magician* comes from the root word Magi, who were the three wise men who read the signs of the heavens, which led them to seek and find a new-born savior and give rise to an entirely new religion. Magic in those days was a sacred art used to work with the powers of nature.

The natural rhythms of the Earth, Sun and Moon influenced the tides, weather and growing seasons and people's very survival often relied on the timely and accurate predictions of these natural patterns. Plant your precious last seeds too early, then suffer a late freeze just as your crop begins to sprout, and it could mean some seriously hard times for you and yours in the months ahead. These patterns of nature were understood to extend far beyond agriculture into all matters of life, love and wellbeing.

There are two main concepts, that the ancient practitioners of Pagan Magic understood, that can be applied to our modern Law of Attraction journey toward our intended results. For centuries these ideas were kept secret and hidden among the few. Initially, these concepts remained hidden simply because they were only passed from master to apprentice in the alchemical laboratories and torch-lit libraries of the most secluded wizards of the age. Eventually, this knowledge was kept secret by the initiated out of fear of persecution and through outright repression by those in authority.

The simple fact is this knowledge was considered a threat to the establishment because if anyone could create and achieve their own accomplishments then there would be no need for a caste system, a religious hierarchy or a governing monarchy. At the same time, if someone were accused then convicted of "unnatural magic" or "witchcraft" then their land could be seized and often was offered as a reward to the accuser. Couple that tidy system with the concept of a "state religion" where the state also controlled an army with the authority to kill anyone who didn't jive with the "official religion" as it were, and you can see how some useful old folk magic might quickly fall out of favor.

Don't worry though. These two secrets of ancient magic don't involve cauldrons or broomsticks. They are nothing more than two ways of looking at the natural world's energies that correspond to our human traits.

The first secret is the concept of the elements. When I was in junior high school I remember a science teacher explaining the periodic table of elements and all its myriad of notations. This science teacher added that in the Dark Ages, people believed that there were only four elements, and he scoffed at their ignorance. It was only years later that I discovered that these early men of science were using the term *element* to describe a phenomenon of Earthly and humanitarian energies. In that ancient system, these four elements are not the same as the chemical constituents that we divide the physical world's components into on the periodic table. They are the essence of life's experience and are thought to represent the various aspects of energy in the human condition as it relates to the natural world.

These four elements are Earth, Air, Fire and Water.

A pure materialist reading that a Medieval tinkerer believed the entire world to be *made up* of these four elements would simply discount the idea and go on to study the fifty million additional elements in his text book. However, these *elements* are more akin to specific energies than physical building blocks. Air represents the energy of our thoughts, our clear ideas and our inspiration. Fire represents our actions, passions, enthusiasms, and creative works of pleasure and joy. Water represents our emotions and feelings, our laughter and tears. And finally, the Earth element represents our physical bodies, our homes and our sacred places. The goal of the ancient magician was to seek a balance among these *elements*.

To me, this system is such an elegant, beautiful way of managing your way in the world that I am amazed it isn't taught to every man woman and child from birth. Consider some of your most challenging and difficult experiences. Chances are that those situations resulted from an imbalance in one of these forces, like giving too much attention and energy to any one of them, or neglecting another. For example, giving all of your attention to thoughts, and never taking actions, or always acting without thinking first. It is a worthy goal to seek balance among these elemental energies. We often hear that the truest way is the way of balance, but for me that has always begged the question: balance of what?

Ancient Secrets of Magic

Well, balance among your thoughts, actions, feelings and physical existence would seem to be a pretty wise place to begin. And what is it that the ancient magicians tell us unites these four elements as a unified system? What is it that moves them in harmony according to the old secret knowledge? Spirit. That higher power that is beyond our mere human intellect, yet that is also an undeniable part of it. So the first ancient secret of magic is that your thoughts, actions, emotions and body should receive equal attention and care so that you may live in harmony and balance while uniting with that Great Spirit which moves us all from the tiniest atom to the grandest Universe as a whole.

The second ancient secret of magic is what is known as the magician's code. In short the magician's code is stated as such: *To Know. To Will. To Dare. To Keep Silent.* As a student of the Law of Attraction, the first time I read this, I was astounded. I made the Law of Attraction correlations right away.

To know is to know what it is that you want. This exactly describes the power of the ideal desired result. First you must know what it is that you intend to accomplish. This is the deliberate part of being a Deliberate Creator.

The second line, *to will* means to give your intention your attention. This is the *thoughts become things* and the *what you give your attention to expands* piece. This also carries with it a veiled warning. Your will is yours alone. No one else is involved at this stage, so be careful what you wish for because you just might get it. That is why *to know* comes before this step, because *to know* also means *to be sure*.

The third line of the ancient magician's code is *to dare*. To dare means to actually do something about it. In other words you must dare to take action toward your goal and you must dare to believe it can be done. It could be said also, that you must dare to act as if it were already true, and you must finally dare to expect it.

The final line is *to keep silent*. Wow. In our modern world of social media, smart phones, and email keeping silent is not a virtue that is often celebrated (unfortunately). Do you have the discipline to actually keep silent about your highest goals and plans? Some would say the more people you tell, the more that shows your belief in yourself and at a certain point that may be true. But I think that in the ancient secret magician's code, *to keep silent* refers to that time when your goal is still a precious infant. It is growing. It must be cultivated and nurtured. Anyone without the most imaginative vision would not recognize its potential at such an embryonic stage. Therefore it would be wise to keep silent about it and allow it to grow.

Sticking to that can be one of the most difficult

disciplines imaginable, but the more I realize the benefits of it, the easier it becomes. In fact, for me it is one of the most treasured aspects of my character that I would be able to pour hours, days and even years of work into something creative, while never so much as chatting about it once. There is something sacred that happens when you *keep silent* about those things that require a long creative process to materialize.

Doing so can protect your most treasured goals and intentions from the petty energies of negative people. You may share some of your endeavors with fellow creatives or those whom you know will support your efforts, but only you will know whom to trust with your dreams. In the end, it is their life and accomplishment that truly matter.

So to apply the ancient secrets of magic remember to seek balance in your Earth/Body, Air/Thought, Fire/Action and Water/Emotion while honoring your individual Spirit as well as the greater universal Spirit that ties these energies together.

Then remember the magician's code: *To Know. To Will. To Dare. To Keep Silent.*

chapter 11

Summary And Conclusion

The Law of Attraction is always working. The question is are you working it? Deliberate Creation is the proactive application of the Law of Attraction. It's *working it* so to speak. It is the deliberate navigation toward your results, your accomplishments and, indeed, your entire life.

As a Deliberate Creator you become an adventurer in the literal sense. You are continually defining ideal desired results that you have never experienced before, then heading out to make them so.

In the romantic days of high exploration early explorers discovered that an ocean current circulated from Europe, across the Atlantic, up the Coast of North America then back across the sea to Europe again. This

Gulfstream current, as we know it today, always existed, whether or not anyone was aware of it. Innovative navigators, ship's captains and crews of *brave, young thoughtless men* (as an old seafaring song puts it) sailed across the ocean and explored an unknown world. Just like this flowing ocean current, the Law of Attraction has always been there, taking you to the places that follow your most oft repeated thoughts and beliefs. The opportunity you have, as a Deliberate Creator, is to use that current to your advantage. The old-time explorers set out (I would wager) as much for the journey as for the destination. Imagine the things they encountered. They saw things wondrous to tell that filled them with awe and elation. And they persisted far beyond the edges of hardship and toil, to places where comfort and pleasure lived only as bitter memories.

The fact is your Deliberate Creation adventures will be just as thrilling and filled with unexpected twists of good luck, mistakes and general craziness. Many say that the final result will never be exactly as you imagined but it will always be to your highest benefit. I say sometimes the end result is precisely the way you imagined it. Not always, but often. One thing is for certain. It beats the Hell out of stumbling along wondering how things will turn out. As someone who proactively navigates the Law of Attraction, there are many times that will challenge you. Your mission is to faithfully follow the process of manifestation.

Deliberate Creators have discovered that thoughts become things. Then millions of people have given it a try, thought about their perfect goal a few times, seen no change and gone back to their everyday life of creating by default. This level of living is confirmed by their surroundings and validated by consensus.

The catch is, to actively realize that thoughts become things, you have to stick to it for long enough. Thoughts of your ideal desired result fully achieved vibrate at a higher frequency than doubt or fear (if feeling better can be described as being higher than feeling worse). Once you sustain such a high vibration for long enough, high power thoughts will be what you go to first. Then your automatic thoughts join you at that high level. You live there. You live in that beautiful place of knowing you can accomplish anything you choose. The time it takes will be different for every person and for every circumstance or goal you reach toward. One clue that you are making headway is the feeling of alignment.

Alignment, as pertains to the Law of Attraction, is that experience when your thoughts, beliefs and actions are all moving together in the same direction as your intentions. Being in alignment is just like being in love or in an athletic, creative or intellectual *zone*. No one can coach you into it, and no one can stop you once you are there. You can't buy the exhilaration of sheer alignment. As time goes on and you become better at finding that place of aligned thought, feeling and action, you will become accustomed to living at that level and you will be amazed at how rapidly some intentions materialize. When you are just starting out, those first moments of alignment will fill you with a surge of energy unlike any other.

One instance I remember clearly was when I first started to write my live music column for the newspaper. It had been my intention to make a living writing for some time. I was still employed at my corporate management job with Starbucks, but on this particular day I was off. I parked downtown to have lunch. After I was done I walked across the street to a new club in town to speak to the owner about the live music dates they were booking for the near future. After that meeting I decided to walk over to another place that had just opened. The day was sunny and clear and walking downtown was quite pleasant. At a certain point in my walk I was overwhelmed with a feeling I can only describe as pure happiness, but that doesn't quite do it justice. The feeling was elation and I felt as if I were walking a foot off the ground. The entire Universe was humming and I was beyond thrilled simply because I was walking to speak to someone about an article I was going to write and be paid for. I was, in that moment, a published, professional writer.

What I wanted, what I deserved, what I was good at, and what I was physically doing were in complete alignment. I have never forgotten that feeling and I draw upon it when I feel tired or less than enthusiastic about writing or doing anything that my writing and publishing business demands at the time.

For years I had hesitated to begin a writing career because I simply did not know how. I did not know where to begin. It was only when I began to consciously give more attention to my ideal desired result (being a writer) than to worrying about not knowing exactly how to do it, that opportunities began to arise. I wrote out my goal as if it were already done, read it every day, and pictured myself working as a completely self-employed writer. When I would have to work my day job, I would take breaks and read my goals to be a writer until I believed them with pure faith, even if they contradicted my surroundings in that moment. On my days off I would take my laptop to the bookstore and work in the café and look at the thousands of books on the shelves. I would say to myself, *every single one of these books were written by someone just like me who at some time in their life had never published a book.* I would work as if that were my only job, and on those days it was. When an opportunity presented itself to write a column I went after it with all of the professionalism and enthusiasm that I could find within myself. Was I trying to publish a novel? Yes. But any writing job was a step in that direction and I took that action to the best of my ability. Keep in mind that I have never stopped studying writing since I began to do so in college. In short, I was prepared. I had defined my ideal desired result to be a writer, focused the majority of my intention on being that successfully and exclusively, visualized myself living in abundance from it, affirmed it until I was dizzy and acted like I already was that every time I had the chance. Then I jumped at the opportunities that were in the same ballpark. Doing so put me in the position to take the Clear Actions toward writing for money (any amount of money) and following my intuition paid off in the craziest ways.

Now I am a full-time writer. I have three books completed, three more outlined and I still write the live music column that got me started because doing it is so much fun.

This story illustrates our four stages of Deliberate Creation. Others have called it many things, and given the process one fewer or one more step, but my definition is the one that I have found, through direct experience, to be the most logical and easy to apply. These four stages of Deliberate Creation as we have managed to arrange them in this book are Destination, Visualization, Affirmations and Actions.

Initially you must chart your course by positively identifying your Destination. This course-charting phase is the definition of your ideal desired result. Then you must believe that you can make it before you ever set sail. Employ your maps and navigational tools to visualize yourself pulling into the ports of your highest goals. Confirm your success by affirming it and give the majority of your thoughts to a perfectly fulfilled destiny. When you have this mental picture in place, step aboard with your obvious, intuitive and *as if* actions. Along the journey remember that doldrums are times to prepare and refocus on your Destination. Tolerate no mutinies, neither by the shortsightedness of others, nor of yourself.

As you take actions be prepared to receive your intention along the way. It may come in pieces. It may come in unexpected emails, phone calls, or conversations. It is openness to your goal that allows it to join you in reality. Receiving is the icing on the Deliberate Creation cake. I really don't list it as a stage in the process because receiving just happens in the moment. You don't plan for it. You don't chase it. You welcome it. You celebrate it. Use it as a firm victory to stand upon and look back over your process.

Remember when your intention was just a thought.

Remember visualizing it before you lived it. Remember affirming it and those moments when it started to change from *maybe* into *definitely* deep inside your mind. Recall your first action steps and how tenuous they felt. Then recall how confidently you stepped toward your goal near the end. As you reflect, understand this: you can do anything.

Links

Take a Little Link Trip:

Please **Review this book here**:
amazon.com/dp/B00K2DS7MI

Your feedback helps me as well as other readers!
Don't be shy… go review this book today!

FREE Weekly Newsletter at espressoforyourgoals.com

Sign up for The FREE weekly newsletter! It's short & sweet, and includes Law of Attraction and Goal Setting Insider Tips, Motivation, and Cool Quotes to Share! We only send it out once a week (on Mondays).

Les Goodrich on Twitter = @LesGoodrich

Follow me on Twitter to get the good stuff
in 160 characters or less!

Visit and Like our EFYG **Facebook Page** at:
facebook.com/espressoforyourgoals

Links

Get the book "Espresso For Your Goals" here:
amazon.com/dp/B00IQBLGIU/

Get it now *so you can* combine
the Law of Attraction with Goal Setting!

Watch the **Free Affirmations Video** here:
http://youtu.be/s6A_1Uo6M18

It's 20 minutes of relaxing music and awesome
pics, plus 100 or so unique, positive affirmations.
Watch the video or just listen, but either way, go dig it.
The Free Affirmations Video is my way to say
Thank you for buying this book!

Vsit the **Les Goodrich Amazon Author Page** here:
amazon.com/Les-Goodrich/e/B00IQFEWQY/
For all of my books on Amazon, plus
Twitter feeds and blog posts all in one place.

Exciting Video Course Offer

If you would like to supercharge your goal setting system further, in more detail and through the magic of the **Espresso For Your Goals Video Course**, simply visit this website address to gain access to the Video Course Members Area:
http://espressoforyourgoals.com/video-course-member-access/

Yes it is something I am selling, but it's a serious value, and it's really cool too. Plus visiting the website just lets you check out the page where you can choose to buy the course or not—No Obligation.

Here is what you will find inside:

> *A series of **FIVE Video Modules** where each topic in the *Espresso For Your Goals System* is *coached in detail* with *examples* and *easy-to-follow instructions* and *Tips!*
>
> ***A Printable Workbook** designed specifically for use in conjunction with the Video Modules.
>
> ***Pure Affirmations Audio / Video**: An Audio Recording of Pure Affirmations with cool pictures and super-chill background music that is exceedingly motivational and powerful.

Exciting Video Course Offer

***FREE BONUS #1:** The <u>*"To Manifest Abundant Wealth"* Mind Movie Video</u> I created for myself, and now you can use it too.

***FREE BONUS #2:** <u>The Mentor Book</u> process revealed! This is a powerful motivational tool that I invented and have never shared with anyone before. This one tool has helped me out of some sticky situations, and it is yours free, as my way of saying *thank you* when you purchase the <u>**Espresso For Your Goals Video Course!**</u>

I could easily sell the video modules and workbook alone for about $50 on clickbank (and someday I might). So why don't I, you ask? Because for now I am more interested in writing than Internet Marketing. Besides, I created this course to offer **even more depth** and **result-generating value** *for you*, the person cool enough and persistent enough to buy, read and use my book. When I priced the <u>**Espresso For Your Goals Video Course**</u> offer, my goal was to create a video course with enough value and free bonuses to be worth easily ***triple the price*** I would sell it for. I fully believe that I have met or exceeded that goal.

Exciting Video Course Offer

This powerful and fun **Espresso For Your Goals Video Course** is available for **one single payment** of **only $27.**

(This price is subject to change and will likely increase with subsequent updates of this book and the video course itself. However, if you find the video course price on the link page is higher than the price shown above, simply email us your purchase receipt with date and we will honor the lowest price. Thank you.)

Now I put a lot more work into it than that, because that is just kind of the way I am (as you may have figured out by now). Think about it: how do you feel about the content and value in this book, compared to the price you spent to get it? So as a result of my overachiever personality, you are assured to get much more value out of the video course than the small, more than fair price of $27. But even so, it still comes with my solid money-back guarantee. **

** My *solid money-back guarantee* is this: If you are not completely satisfied with the **Espresso For Your Goals Video Course** product once you have purchased it and genuinely tried it, just let me know and I will refund your money 100%, no questions asked. –Les Goodrich.

So just ***visit the website address below*** to get the **Espresso For Your Goals Video Course**, and I will see you inside the course Members Area. Rock On!

http://espressoforyourgoals.com/video-course-member-access/

www.ingramcontent.com/pod-product-compliance
Lightning Source LLC
Chambersburg PA
CBHW031359040426
42444CB00005B/356